THE JAIL THAT WENT TO SEA

THE
JAIL
THAT WENT
TO SEA

*An Untold Story of the Battle
of the Atlantic, 1941–42*

PETER HAINING

ROBSON BOOKS

First published in Great Britain in 2003 by Robson Books,
The Chrysalis Building, Bramley Road, London, W10 6SP

A member of **Chrysalis** Books plc

940.5452
HAI

The photographs and illustrations in this book are from the W.O.G.
Lofts' Archive, Imperial War Museum, Cassell & Company and the
author's own collection.

The author has made every reasonable effort to contact all copyright
holders. Any errors that may have occurred are inadvertent and
anyone who for any reason has not been contacted is invited to write
to the publishers so that a full acknowledgement may be made in
subsequent editions of this work.

British Library Cataloguing in Publication Data
A catalogue record for this title is available from the British Library.

ISBN 1 86105 561 7

Index prepared by Indexing Specialists (UK) Ltd.
Typeset by FiSH Books, London W1
Printed in Great Britain by Creative Print & Design (Wales),
Ebbw Vale

In memory of
W.O.G. LOFTS
who first investigated the story

Contents

Author's Note

In order to protect the identities of the relatives of a number of the men featured in this narrative, some of the names have been changed. In every other aspect it is a true story.

Peter Haining
London, March 2003

Foreword

In the autumn of 1941, the people of Britain had their backs to the wall in their lone fight against the might of Hitler's Germany. America was then still neutral – although the North American continent as a whole had become a vital element in the supply of materials and food to the beleaguered nation. Between the two countries lay the fastness of the Atlantic Ocean where German battleships and 'Wolf Packs' of U-boats patrolled the storm-tossed waters looking for their victims, unarmed merchant ships laden with precious cargoes.

Yet in Glasgow – one end of this crucial link – a particular facet of life remained unchanged. The city was still widely known as the 'gangster capital of the British Isles' and, despite a concerted campaign by the police in the thirties, there were still defiant mobs of gangsters such as the Billy Boys and Norman Conks, both from Bridgeton. Both were deeply involved in crime and violence, their minds more set on inter-necine warfare than on the life or death struggle taking place with the Nazis.

Then, one day, some of these unregenerate hoodlums became the object of an extraordinary recruitment campaign and found themselves part of one of the strangest episodes of Second World War history.

11

Because of the mounting numbers of merchant ships being lost to enemy action as they crossed the Atlantic – and the inevitable rising death toll of merchant seamen – desperate measures were required to keep the crucial lifeline operational. Able-bodied men *had* be found, it was decided by the naval authorities under pressure from the War Office, even, if necessary, from the ranks of known criminals and ex-convicts. And what better place to start than in Glasgow, the focal point of the link to North America?

This is the story of how one ship went to sea with a crew including men whose lives had been steeped in lawlessness. Men who, in most cases, had never been to sea before and resented authority in all forms. Their ship, the *George Washington*, was to prove just as unusual as the crew: a former German luxury liner that had once been sabotaged by its seamen and had since lain forgotten for years in an American backwater.

It is a story that has not been told in full before. A story that combines the violent and dangerous underworld of Glasgow half a century ago with the bravery of those who sailed on merchant ships during the bloody Battle of the Atlantic. The fact that it *can* be told now owes much to the work carried out by the late historian, W. O. G. Lofts, a man of great dedication and resourcefulness, who was once described by the author Leslie Charteris, of *The Saint* fame, as 'a man who always gets to the facts' and by the *Independent* as 'one of the great researchers of the century'.

When Lofts, who had been a friend of mine for many years, died in 1997, he bequeathed to me his extensive archive of papers. Among these I found a file of material devoted to the *George Washington*. He had obviously been fascinated by the unique story of this ship and her motley crew. As well as gathering copies of a large number of references, diary entries, newspaper cuttings from the thirties and forties, and documents finally de-restricted by the Public Records Office in

London, he had made contact with several of the merchant seamen involved in the saga. Their memories helped to add the human element to the more staid official reports.

Sadly, Lofts' death meant his research was left incomplete. But the story so gripped my imagination as I read through the file that I decided to continue the investigation he had started. This account of the jail that went to sea is the result and it is dedicated to him because without him it would never have been written.

Chapter 1

Navy Press Gang – 1941 Style

The looming fortress of Barlinnie Jail was silent and still as dawn broke over the city of Glasgow on the morning of 15 August 1941. It had rained during the night and the streets around the massive building glistened in the first sunlight of the day. A small mongrel dog padded past the prison's large, iron-studded gates and somewhere in the distance the sound of the engine of a solitary motor vehicle could be heard approaching.

Although the prison had been built only a little over half a century earlier, there was something solid and enduring about its appearance that seemed to mirror the circumstances under which it had been erected. In the 1870s there had been a considerable demand for prison accommodation to be provided in the east of Glasgow – the western district already had its own jail – but because of the large-scale mining operations that had been carried out all over the district during the preceding years there was very little suitable land left.

In response to public pressure, though, a careful survey was carried out in the area by the local authority. Finally, a site of just over 32 acres, which formed a part of the large Barlinnie farm estate on the Cumbernauld Road and was bounded on the north by the Monkland canal, was deemed suitable. It was duly purchased by HM Prison Commissioners and building work began almost at once. The elevated position meant that the new jail would not be overlooked by any future buildings, and there was easy road access to the city centre just over two miles away.

The quarries of whinstone rock in the area meant that the basic raw materials for the construction were to hand and by the following summer the first block of the new prison had been completed. A wharf on the canal was opened, providing an ideal point for landing materials. (This would later prove useful for carrying various commodities between the city and the prison when it was fully operational.)

Barlinnie Jail finally received its first prisoners on 15 August 1882. By a curious coincidence, on this same day almost sixty years later the events began that would go down in the history of naval warfare as the saga of the jail that went to sea.

On the morning of 15 August 1941, the huge prison gates swung open once again. This time, though, they were opening to *release* a group of men, who stumbled out into the street, most of them blinking in the bright daylight. Their voices, rowdy and thick with the accents of slumland Glasgow, cut through the stillness as, one by one, they drew deep breaths of fresh air and savoured the scent of freedom.

Also, by another coincidence, the names of some of these men were a reminder of landmarks in the history of Barlinnie Jail. In 1889, for example, the first convict to escape from the prison had been a man named Wilson, who had climbed over a wall near the canal, only to be captured by the police the following day and returned to his cell. Thirty years later, another inmate, McCormack, while on transfer from Polmont Institution, escaped from his escort at Glasgow Railway Station, but was also soon recaptured.

At Christmas 1934, when Barlinnie had a population of almost 800 men, it made newspaper headlines again. On 22 December, after several days of unrest among the prisoners, a group of between thirty and forty men began smashing up the furniture and glass windows of their cells. A number of warders were called in to try to quell the disturbance and rapidly became involved in a pitched battle that was only stopped by the use of batons, according to a report of the incident in the *Glasgow Daily Record*.

On 25 January, twenty prisoners appeared before the Glasgow Sheriff Court, all of them pleading guilty to charges of causing 'a violent and riotous tumult' and injuring six warders. Eighteen of the men were sentenced to three months' additional imprisonment with hard labour, while the remaining two, named as Corrcoran and Dunn, who had previous convictions for assault, were given six months with hard labour. The *Daily Record* also listed among the other accused the names of John Wilson, Hugh McCormack and John McCourt, all men with records for violence.

Among the men who swaggered through the gates of Barlinnie on that summer morning just six years later – swearing gleefully at the warder who had opened the gates – were another John Wilson, a William McCormack and one Bobbie McCourt, all well-known Glasgow gangsters. Wilson and McCormack belonged to the notorious Billy Boys of Bridgeton, a predominantly Protestant group, and they were accompanied by another member of the gang, Bill Fullerton, who had been imprisoned at the same time.

A few moments later, Bobbie McCourt emerged with a companion, Paddy Mulholland. They belonged to a rival Bridgeton gang, the Norman Conks, mostly Roman Catholics. It had been the bitter rivalry between these two mobs of hardmen – whose religious affiliations were among the least of their differences, as they rarely, if ever, went to church – that had landed all five in Barlinnie three years earlier.

During their time in the jail, McCourt and Mulholland had, for obvious reasons, avoided the trio of Billy Boys whenever possible, and they had no particular desire to confront them now that they were being released. The truth is, though, that not one of the ill-assorted group of five ex-cons could possibly have imagined what fate held in store for them in the next eighteen months. For these fiercest of enemies were all destined to share in a unique naval odyssey on the high seas that would take them across the U-boat-infested Atlantic Ocean and into action on a run-down, former German liner that had long ago been laid up from maritime service . . .

The engine of the motor vehicle that had disturbed the early morning quiet of the Cumbernauld Road had now fallen silent and disgorged six grumbling men into the street. None of them was overly enthusiastic about making such an early start to their day or about this particular mission – or even about those they would have to deal with. But they were professionals and knew that the war effort required their best efforts.

The men walked quietly towards the bulk of Barlinnie and heard the voices of those they had come to see moments before they actually saw them. The biggest of the group, a man with close-cropped, steel-grey hair, wearing a raincoat over his broad shoulders, indicated that the other five should spread themselves across the road as their quarry swung into view.

For a moment, the group of a dozen men just released from Barlinnie and the six newcomers stood quite still and eyed one another. It might almost have been a scene from the kind of Western film that the gangsters liked watching. Recognition was instantaneous on both sides.

'It's thae busies, the fooking bastards,' a voice among the ex-prisoners swore.

A twisted smile spread across the tough face of the big man in the raincoat. 'Well, what a sight first thing in the morning!' he said in an accent that was unmistakably Yorkshire. 'We want a word with you, lads.'

As the six men divided the muttering jailbirds into pairs, the man in the raincoat crooked his finger knowingly at John Wilson and William McCormack. Wilson recognised an old adversary at once. Even after three years inside, he instantly knew the scarred face of the policeman who had hounded him for years in Bridgeton and finally put him away. Sergeant Joseph Robinson of the Glasgow gang-busting squad.

The fact that Robinson was not a Scot had made him stand out from the local policemen right from the start. He had come from Sheffield where he had been something of a legend in the battle with that city's notorious gangsters. The scars on his weathered face and jaw were the evidence of a vicious attack when four thugs had set upon him as he was entering a shop and left him maimed and covered with razor slashes.

The beating, though, had served only to make Sergeant Robinson all the more determined to bring down the Sheffield 'razor gangsters', hoodlums who had emerged in the early twenties following a gang murder in the Attercliffe district. The city had become increasingly plagued by violence and crime with the gangsters showing an almost complete disregard for the law.

Armed only with a long wooden staff and accompanied by a hand-picked team of fellow officers as steely as himself, Robinson had taken on the toughs at every opportunity – no matter that they often carried razors and sometimes even swords and axes. With the knowledge and backing of their divisional superintendent, the sergeant and his men dished out their own brand of justice on the mean streets of Sheffield: often meeting coshes and knives with bare fists, but never pulling back from a fight and rapidly gaining a reputation as a no-nonsense squad.

Sergeant Robinson's success in Sheffield had led his boss, Chief Constable Percy Sillitoe, to bring him to Glasgow when he was moved on to combat the Scottish city's even more violent gangs. Here, a similarly hard-nosed campaign in the years preceding the Second World War had drastically reduced the crime rate and put many of the most brutal gangsters into prison.

'Weil, if it's no Sergeant Robinson. What are ye an aw they *jailers* [plain clothes men] doin' aboot at this time of morning?' Despite his tone, there was a hint of respect in John Wilson's voice.

'Enjoy your holiday in Barlinnie, Wilson?' Robinson quipped, pulling the lapels of his coat a little tighter over the familiar copper's light blue shirt and black tie. 'Because you're going to miss it where you're going. I want a word before you get on the drink again.'

The mention of drink brought a smile to the face of the other man, William McCormack. Known as a notorious boozer before his latest imprisonment, McCormack had already expressed his intention of going on a bender as soon as he was free. He had no liking for the police and said so before Robinson could continue.

'Away an pap shite at the moon,' he said, uttering a familiar piece of Glasgow abuse towards the police, and was about to brush past the sergeant. Robinson might have been responsible for putting him and the others away, but he had done his time in the *peter* and was not going to stand around listening to another lecture as soon as he was released.

McCormack knew all about there being a war on, but he reckoned that the old pleasures of booze and screwing would be around for the smart *Glesga* boy who knew where to look. The *shebeen* on London Road where drinks flowed at any hour of the day or night; the kip shops in Bridgeton where a man could *beef* a bit of young stuff for a few shillings; and the single-end on Abercromby Road where the next bit of villainy to get some *dough* could be planned – Hitler or no bloody Hitler.

20

'You'll listen to *me*,' Robinson said firmly, pushing McCormack back with the palms of his hands. 'Or you'll both be back inside before your throats are wet!'

The look in the sergeant's eyes told Wilson and McCormack that he was not joking. Around them, the other ex-cons had also stopped their banter and were listening to what they were being told.

Sergeant Robinson had, in fact, already delivered the same message earlier in the week to another group of criminals just released from Barlinnie. This morning, though, was slightly different in that he had known Wilson and McCormack on the streets of Bridgeton, and had been one of the officers who had arrested them along with Fullerton and the two Norman Conks, Bobbie McCourt and Paddy Mulholland, for causing an affray on Glasgow Green.

That had been three years ago, but already it seemed like an incident from an age that had passed. The five men had been given longer prison sentences than usual for the offence because of their records of violence and, in the interim, gangsters had lost much of their hold on slumland Glasgow. The advent of war in the autumn of 1939 had further accelerated this decline.

Sergeant Robinson felt he could get straight to the point of this early morning encounter. The task that had been entrusted to him and his officers was to find crew members for the merchant navy. The Battle of the Atlantic had been taking a terrible toll in ships and seamen since the start of the war. German U-boats were ruling the ocean between Europe and America – just as the German Army was now in control of much of Europe – and if supplies could not be got through to the beleaguered British Isles from the USA, then the war would surely be lost.

The directive to find crews for the merchant ships had come through from the War Office in London. Men were to be recruited from among the city's floating population with as few questions asked as possible. Able-bodied and willing if possible; if they were unwilling, then with a degree of persuasion at the officers' discretion.

It was considered to be an opportunity with obvious attractions to certain types of men at loose in Glasgow. Men such as army deserters sheltering behind forged identity cards, or criminals hunted by the law. It was perhaps somewhat less attractive to villains being released back into society after serving their time. But these were desperate times and such men did, after all, represent a new pool of labour – though of what calibre it was impossible to guess.

The mission had taken Robinson and his team from one side of Glasgow's underworld to the other. From the Gorbals pubs to the gambling dens in Cowcaddens and the drinking shops in Argyle Street. Now it was the turn of Barlinnie.

Their objective this August morning was crew for a specific ship – a one-time luxury cruise liner, the *George Washington*, which was being loaned by the American government for use as a British troopship – for which 500 men were required. The numbers were growing steadily, but not as .quickly as the authorities in London would like. The pressure was on Robinson and his officers as they confronted their latest 'prospects' outside Barlinnie Jail.

'I know you like a fight,' the sergeant grinned at Wilson and McCormack after he had outlined the facts. 'So you just sign on and do your bit for your country. But if you don't do as I say, I'll see you're back inside in no time. And that goes for all of this lot.'

'Fook ye, Robinson, that's blackmail,' Wilson exploded. 'I'm no afrighted of a *ba'le*, but ye'll have tae put me in a *cairt* [Black Maria] afore I'll go tae sea.'

'You're on!' said Robinson thrusting his scarred face menacingly into Wilson's.

The exuberant mood of all the men who had left Barlinnie just a short while ago now began to evaporate as the significance of what they had been told sank in. There was no mistaking the threat implicit in what the sergeant and the others were saying. This was wartime and it seemed obvious that the coppers were going to crew the merchant ships any damn way they could.

It probably did not occur to any of the men that the proposition – such as it was – amounted to press-gang tactics. Certainly, such a style of unequivocal 'recruitment' had not been used to crew British ships since the days of Lord Nelson more than 150 years earlier. The facts have, not surprisingly, remained something of a secret in merchant navy history until now and have only come to light as a result of painstaking research into naval archives and press files as well as the recollections of those few people still alive who knew and worked alongside the five battling gangsters from Bridgeton who went to war at sea.

The event that had brought the five men, Wilson, McCormack, Fullerton, McCourt and Mulholland, together at this turning point in their lives had occurred three years earlier on a Sunday morning on Glasgow Green. The month was July, at the end of the Glasgow Fair fortnight, and the year was 1938.

The Green is the city's most frequented open area and lies just across the Clyde from the Gorbals. It is a triangular patch of park situated between the St Andrew's and King Street bridges, and by 1938 had for years been a focal point for young people from the slums as well as a battle ground for warring gangsters looking for a *sherricking*.

McCourt and Mulholland had been lounging on the grass drinking bottles of beer when the three Billy Boys, Wilson, McCormack and Fullerton, had seen them as they were walking by along King's Drive. The fact that the pair of Norman Conks were at a numerical disadvantage was too good an opportunity for their enemies to resist. It was John Wilson who yelled out the traditional taunt of a Protestant to Catholic rivals, 'God save the King!' following this with a stream of obscenities about the Norman Conks' parentage and sexual proclivities and a challenge, 'Got the *crap* on?' When McCourt and Mulholland stood up and began to return the abuse and the two groups closed in on each other, a fight was inevitable.

According to a report of the subsequent trial of the five men in the *Glasgow Herald*, the sight of them laying into each other with fists, knives and broken beer bottles sent members of the public scurrying from the Green. The police were called and soon the familiar figure of Sergeant Robinson and two of his gang-busters were endeavouring to separate the bloody and bruised combatants.

So deep was the enmity between the rival factions of gangsters, however, that fists flew in all directions. During their attempts to separate the men, two of the policeman had their faces slashed by bottles and Sergeant Robinson himself received a number of blows to the head. Finally, the arrival at the Green of one of the city's radio-controlled police cars with two more officers enabled them to stop the brawling and arrest all five participants, according to the *Herald*.

The trial proceedings in the Glasgow Sheriff Court, at which Robinson was the prosecution's chief witness, merited only a few paragraphs in the local press – now rather more concerned with the gathering threat of Nazi Germany than with a bit of internecine scrapping between gangsters. The papers reported that all five men were found guilty of causing an affray and assaulting police officers. When told of the accused men's lengthy criminal records, the magistrate, Bailie McLean, passed sentences of three years' imprisonment on each of them.

Although the details of the men's criminal records were not given in the *Glasgow Herald*'s account of the trial, they make

24

for colourful reading and help to flesh out the characters of the quintet of press-ganged seamen.

When they were arrested, John Wilson and William McCormack were both tall, dark-haired, muscular 21-year-olds from Abercromby Street, the heart of Billy Boy territory in Bridgeton. Born just at the end of the First World War, they had grown up in squalor, their fathers neglectful, brawling, heavy drinkers whose only contributions to their sons' upbringing had been regular beatings and an encouragement to violence and theft.

The lads' criminal records ran almost in parallel. As youngsters, both John and William had 'dain ma *hoosey* fur screwin' hooses' [served time at approved schools for house-breaking] and as teenage recruits to the Billy Boys had several times been 'up for R and D' [charged with riot and disorder]. Their indoctrination into the violent culture and religious bigotry of the gang had actually been sealed when as fifteen-year-olds, they were involved in a famous pitched battle in 1932 between the Billy Boys and Norman Conks in Abercromby Street.

Wilson grew to boast of his dexterity with a knife and his influence on other members of the Billy Boys. He was widely considered to be one of the gangsters or 'flymen' and '*dead thick*' a local term meaning wide awake and knowing. In Bridgeton it was said he had a natural way of leading others on and could be quite vain.

For years, in fact, Wilson, like any number of small-time gangsters with a craving for publicity, carried a newspaper cutting in his pocket that he said had been written by a reporter from the Glasgow *Sunday Mail* who had spoken to him during an investigation into crime in Glasgow. The story, dated 3 February 1935, read:

During the past ten years, in Glasgow alone, gangsterdom has been responsible for at least four slayings and the

25

serious injuring and maiming of many others who have incurred the savage wrath of the different cliques of young hooligans who terrorise the poorer districts of the city.

The true trysting places of the gangsters are the cheap dance halls, dens of obscene morality, that exist in many parts of the city. In true Chicago style, the Glasgow gangster has his 'Moll' and in these dance halls she is frequently the cause of the trouble that leads to razor-slashed faces and bottle-crowned heads.

Wilson's friend, William McCormack, had grown up to love the bottle as much as he hated his Catholic-sounding surname. Quick to anger and marked with the scars of innumerable dance-hall fights and skirmishes with rival hoodlums, he preferred to be known to one and all by the single name, 'Wull'. His brand of brutality made him attractive to girls, and he had fathered two illegitimate children before being imprisoned in 1938.

Bill Fullerton, the third Billy Boy, claimed to be related to the legendary founder of the Billy Boys, William Fullerton, but a reputation of being quick to anger and a bit of a liar, which had followed him from childhood, tended to undermine his boasting. Rather scrawny, with watery blue eyes and sandy hair, he was, nonetheless, a loyal member of the gang and as a child had run errands – including 'holding the *bag* [money]' – for several of the razor kings who dominated the hierarchy during the late twenties and early thirties.

The young Fullerton loved the cinema and particularly enjoyed the American gangster films that flooded into the cinemas of Glasgow after the release in 1930 of the hugely successful *Little Caesar* starring Edward G Robinson as the small-time gangster who makes good. Fullerton often boasted that one day he would own a 'Tommy Gun' like the one Little Rico used in the film.

Local legend identified Fullerton as one of the instigators of a fight in a local cinema that headlined by the *Evening Times*: 'RIOT IN CITY PICTURE HOUSE – GANG WARFARE HELD RESPONSIBLE'. A Superintendent Cameron was quoted as saying, 'The picture house had been singled out latterly by various gangs who deliberately wrecked the performances. Every member of the audience on this occasion was in a state of panic.'

Although the fourth man, Bobbie McCourt, a broad-shouldered figure with watchful dark eyes, had been trailing behind the main group of released prisoners to avoid Wilson, McCormack and Fullerton as they all set off on the hour-long walk to the centre of Glasgow, he was an equally feared member of the Norman Conks with a reputation as a skilled knife fighter. Now aged thirty, he was regarded as something of an old man by some of the gangsters, but the story of his part in the battle of Kerr Street was enough to earn him respect from all but the most foolhardy.

Born in Norman Street, Bridgeton, McCourt had been brought up by a devoted Catholic mother and a wastrel father who deserted the family of three boys and two girls when they were all still youngsters. Despite his mother's attempts to make him a church-goer, Bobbie had fallen under the spell of the Norman Conks and was enjoying the *rammys* [fights] with their rivals as much as anyone. By the age of sixteen he had 'done his *thruple*' [time in junior, intermediate and senior approved schools].

McCourt's favourite weapon had been a Gurkha knife left behind by his errant father which had helped to establish his reputation until he lost the terrifying weapon in the battle of Kerr Street. A report of the events appears in another graphic newspaper cutting from the Glasgow *Evening Times* of 17 June 1931:

The spear of a swordfish and a wicked-looking Gurkha knife were among the number of weapons taken possession of by the police following an alleged gang fight in Kerr Street, Bridgeton, yesterday afternoon. The 'battlefield' was strewn with weapons after the fight including a piece of copper tubing, a brass-headed poker, a cudgel two feet long with a knob of wood as thick as the head of a drumstick, an axe weighing almost two pounds, a steel file two feet long and an iron rod three feet long with a hook at each end. Many of these articles, it is stated, were thrown away by the gangsters in their flight from the police.

Bobbie McCourt always maintained that the Gurkha knife had been wrestled from him by one of the police officers and that far from running away from the police he had beaten one officer unconscious before slipping away through the Calton Burying Ground and walking back home to Norman Street on the south side of Bridgeton.

The fifth man, Paddy Mulholland, who had been arrested with McCourt on Glasgow Green, was some ten years younger and, in the older man's eyes, a bit of a *bam-pot* [fool]. He had been rather keener to take on the three Billy Boys than Bobbie, who knew only too well that his record would not help him when the busies finally bundled all five men into a *cairt*.

Heavily built, with dark, smouldering eyes, Mulholland had been born in Bartholomew Street adjacent to Norman Street and, as was typical of many youngsters in Glasgow at the time, joined the nearest gang for self-protection. Certainly, it didn't pay not to belong to a mob in Bridgeton in the troubled thirties. Being one of the Norman Conks also got Paddy out of the house away from his brutal, alcoholic, Irish-born father and tiny, oppressed mother whose constant fights filled the boy with an urge to leave Bridgeton

Though he, too, enjoyed the violence, thieving and easy sex to be had as one of the Norman Conks, he was immediately attracted by the stories of an uncle who came to visit the family one day and told them all about his life as a merchant seamen. Paddy immediately sensed the chance of a new life. Still only sixteen – but already big for his age, Mulholland managed by his own account to join the crew of a Glasgow merchant ship bound for South Africa. He enjoyed every minute of the trip to Durban, relishing the hard work and companionship of the other seamen. But when the ship docked, and he and the others planned to go ashore, the boy was prevented from doing so because he had 'nae papers'.

It was a sad and angry young man who made the return trip to Glasgow. Within days of arriving in Bridgeton, Paddy Mulholland had fallen in again with the Norman Conks and returned to crime, getting himself arrested initially for fights in dance halls which carried sentences of thirty days – and then graduating to breaking into houses and factories. He had not long finished a six-month sentence in Barlinnie for demanding money with menaces from a shopkeeper before the affray on Glasgow Green saw him back in the same jail for an even longer stay.

The reaction of McCourt and Mulholland to Sergeant Robinson's 'proposal' could not have been more different. Bobbie McCourt had never been further from Glasgow than a boat trip as a child up the River Clyde and was appalled at the idea; Paddy Mulholland could barely restrain a grin. The thought of going back to sea now he was old enough had actually been going through Paddy's mind ever since he had been sent down at the Sheriff Court. And often during his time in Barlinnie he had read admiringly in the newspapers about the merchant seamen taking part in the Battle of the Atlantic.

Paddy Mulholland looked around at the other men on the Cumbernauld Road, all thinking about what they were being told by the policeman, and he let out a sigh of delight. Those other miserable fuckers might not fancy it, but no one

would need to twist his arm to sign on. So there was a
dangerous and bloody war going on at sea? What the hell did
they think had been going on in Glasgow – especially
Bridgeton – for years?

Chapter 2

To Sea in the 'Death Traps'

The Battle of the Atlantic, which had reached such a critical phase in August 1941 that the merchant navy needed to recruit men just released from prison to crew its ships, had been regarded as a crucial element in the British struggle against Germany from the day war broke out. Indeed, the battle would span the entire course of the Second World War and prove vital to Britain's survival and ultimate triumph. The nation's stalwart prime minister, Winston Churchill, never doubted the importance of the events that took place on that great expanse of ocean, writing later in his mammoth history, *The Second World War* (1962):

> The Battle of the Atlantic was the dominating factor all through the war. Never for one moment could we forget that everything happening elsewhere, on land, at sea, or in the air, depended ultimately on its outcome, and amid all other cares, we viewed its changing fortunes day by day with hope or apprehension.

Churchill probably had better reason than most to appreciate the importance of keeping open the routes to the neutral United States after war had been declared in September 1939. He was First Sea Lord at the Admiralty

31

and knew that German U-boats were already patrolling beneath the waves of the Atlantic. The first, brutal sinking of a ship, the 14,000-ton Glasgow-built liner, the *Athenia*, carrying 1,418 passengers including men, women and children heading for Canada, by a torpedo in her port side from U-30 on 3 September – the very day Britain declared war on Germany – highlighted not only how crucial this battle would be, but also how difficult it would be to defeat the relentless and elusive submarines.

With the benefit of hindsight, and the release of classified war-time documents, it is easy to see how quickly Churchill came to realise that Britain had no chance of preventing Germany conquering Europe – probably Britain, too – without the economic, financial and industrial support of the US. It was thanks largely to the 'special relationship' that developed between Churchill and the American President Franklin Delano Roosevelt – who also became convinced that an unchecked Nazi Germany might even one day strike at his own nation – that Britain gained the vital support of the United States.

The fact that 22 American citizens died on the *Athenia* certainly outraged US public opinion and turned up the growing American hostility towards Germany. There was, though, still strong support for isolationism among a number of the Congressmen and several ethnic groups including the 12 million US citizens of German descent and the 15 million Irish Americans. They did not want 'Nazism, Communism, Fascism or even British Imperialism', to quote one commentator, 'They want Americanism.'

In order to survive and fight the war, Britain needed to import every month thousands of tons of raw materials (mainly phosphate, sulphur and cotton) to build and equip ships, aircraft and weapons. North Sea oil had not yet been discovered, so every barrel of oil to fuel the ships, aircraft and tanks had to come from America or the Middle East. Canada was also vital to the equation as a provider of wheat and a variety of manufactured articles not to mention being a place for training soldiers and airmen before they were embarked to the theatres of war in Europe and across the world.

The equally vital supplies of millions of tons of foodstuffs also had to be brought across the Atlantic in merchant ships which from day one were menaced by the bulk of Germany's submarine fleet. A total of 49 U-boats out of 57 were on station on 3 September under the command of the brilliant naval strategist, Admiral Karl Dönitz, a former U-boat captain destined to become commander-in-chief of the *Kriegsmarine* (German Navy). Later still, Dönitz would be appointed by Hitler as his successor shortly before the Führer committed suicide.

From the very start of the war, Dönitz argued that only a naval campaign – and particularly one with submarines – would defeat the United Kingdom. 'The focal point of the war against England and the one possibility of bringing her to her knees lies in attacking sea communications in the Atlantic,' he declared. He estimated that if Germany could destroy between 600,000 and 750,000 tons of British shipping per month for a year, England would sue for peace. For this he would require 300 ocean-going U-boats. Despite this overestimate of the tonnage – further compounded by the decision of Hitler who undoubtedly underestimated the importance of the Battle of the Atlantic until it was too late and provided insufficient submarines to carry out the task – the cross-ocean conflict would still prove to be a near-run thing during the ensuing years.

It had been a fact for some years that Britain produced only enough food to feed half its population, with reserves just enough for a few months, and in the first four months of the war, it became necessary to import 55 million tons of raw materials by sea. The cost of getting these supplies to British ports would prove huge in terms of both shipping and manpower.

Although the German submarines were undoubtedly the biggest threat to merchant shipping, surface raiders including warships and converted merchant ships were also soon accounting for a considerable number of these vessels. The U-boat's most potent weapon of destruction was certainly the torpedo, although they regularly laid mines across the major shipping lanes. Until the summer of 1942, however, the torpedo used by the Germans remained the same model as that developed in the First World War, which had actually to hit its target to activate the firing mechanism and explode. Even allowing for this shortcoming, one mine or torpedo hitting the right place was still capable of sinking the largest ship – a fact that added to the sense of anxiety that every merchant seaman felt on the Atlantic crossings.

Another hangover from the First World War was the use by the U-boats of the 'Wolf Pack' tactics that Dönitz had adopted and renamed *Rudeltaktik* ('Pack Attacks'). These had first been utilised in the Mediterranean and required the submarines to spread out across the convoy routes between Britain and America and then attack when the conditions were most favourable.

To try to thwart these tactics, many of the British merchant ships sailed in convoys escorted by two destroyers. The convoys, normally spread over about 20 square miles of sea, were made up of a maximum of 70 ships, and steamed in a compact formation with each vessel some three and a half cables from the next. Occasionally aircraft of Coastal Command would fly patrols over the convoys in the hope of spotting any lurking U-boats.

Not all of the old sea dogs in the merchant ships found it easy to knuckle down to the rules of the Royal Navy escorts, however: keeping in a certain specified position, avoiding making smoke or dumping rubbish, and not showing lights at night – all, of course, to prevent giving away the convoy's position. Nor were instructions on the complex procedure for zigzagging to make themselves harder to hit, without careering into one another, any better received. Some of the captains firmly believed they knew better how to protect their ships and men, and tensions often simmered as the ships laboured across the storm-tossed Atlantic.

Some of the faster vessels were, though, allowed to travel on their own: a decision made on account partly of pressure from the shipowners and partly because of the shortage of escorts. The lone captains were encouraged by the knowledge that the submerged speed of a U-boat was reckoned to be no faster than that of convoy vessels. On the surface, however, the submarines were quicker than conventional shipping, although vulnerable to being sighted and attacked.

It was the U-boats' capability for surprise when suddenly surfacing from the depths that made them so feared by British seamen. That, and the knowledge that if a submarine missed one ship, the U-boat captain merely needed to wait patiently before another came along as surely as night followed day.

At the start of the war, Britain possessed a fleet of more than 6,000 ocean-going merchant ships and Churchill was desperate that there should not be a repeat of what had happened in the First World War. Working in the Admiralty then, too, he remembered that by the spring of 1917, the success of the U-boat tactics had brought the nation to the edge of defeat. In the blackest month of all, April, one in four ships leaving British ports failed to reach its destination and a massive total of 800,000 tons of shipping was sunk by the submarines.

Churchill recalled vividly that the introduction of the convoy system was the last-ditch solution that proved the nation's salvation. Would it now be the nation's salvation once again, he pondered as the drama in the Atlantic began to unfold?

Just how strong the German determination was to stop the flow of merchant ships can now be judged from a Naval War Staff memorandum dated Berlin, 15 October 1939, which was found in the Nazi war archives. Headed, 'Maritime Requirements for the Decisive Struggle Against Britain,' it read:

Germany's principal enemy in this war is Britain. Her most vulnerable spot is her maritime trade. The principal target of our naval strategy therefore must be the merchant ship, not only the enemy's, but every merchantman which sails the seas in order to supply the enemy's war interests...

Military success can most confidently be expected if we attack British sea communications where they are most accessible to us with the greatest ruthlessness. The final aim of such attacks is to cut off all imports into, and exports from, Britain.

That month of October 1939 saw the figures of German successes rise steeply, with 27 British merchantmen torpedoed and another 19 destroyed by mines laid by the U-boats. Churchill at once took action by deciding to arm a thousand of the merchant ships with twelve-pound guns from a stockpile dating from the First World War. This, he hoped, would force the submarines to operate underwater, as he explained in a memo to the increasingly anxious owners of the merchant fleet: 'The U-boats will not be as successful with underwater attacks – there is nothing like the free play on the surface. So although the war will become more brutal, nevertheless it will be to our advantage.'

Once the Germans became aware of this arming of merchantmen, however, it was seized upon as a *carte blanche* for attacking any armed ship. Some of the shipowners opposed

Churchill's plan in the belief that it actually invited an attack on their ships, although the captains and crews generally welcomed anything that gave them a chance to hit back at the sneaky enemy below the waves.

In the weeks and months that followed this decision, some members of the 'Wolf Packs' occasionally found they had bitten off a little more than they could chew when confronting some of the crews of merchant seamen. In their excellent account of *The Battle of the Atlantic* (1977), John Costello and Terry Hughes have written:

> Accounts of such defiant incidents were circulated to shipping companies to encourage their captains to fight the U-boats. The courage and skill displayed was typical of the resolute way in which the merchant seamen accepted that from now on they were going to be in the front line of the war at sea. The men of the Merchant Navy were a fiercely independent body of civilians who were inclined to refer to their uniformed colleagues as, 'the pansy Royal Navy with its perishing gas and gaiters'.

As Costello and Hughes have also pointed out, the men who sailed under the Red Ensign were often a mixed bunch of nationalities: tough, independent and with little regard for rank. At the start of the war they numbered 120,500 men who together crewed some 6,000 ships over 500 tons which made up the largest merchant marine in the world. Statistics reveal there were 4,500 captains in command of the ships, supported by 20,000 engineers and about 13,000 deck officers.

Of the ordinary seamen, there were 36,000 deck ratings, 30,000 engine-room men and 17,000 stewards. Among their ranks were donkeymen, greasers, stokers, firemen and trimmers who had been drawn from all over the British Empire. Many were indentured seamen from India and alongside them worked stewards from Bombay with Sikhs from the Punjab to be found toiling as stokers in the boiler rooms of the many coal-burning ships.

A lot of these men had been taken on by the shipping companies that plied between their home ports in the tropics and the United Kingdom. With the coming of war, however, the ships were redirected to cross the icy waters of the Atlantic and an already demanding job became fraught with danger. Those merchant seaman employed in the engine room stood little chance when a torpedo struck their ship, and even those Africans and Indians who survived such hits and had to take to the lifeboats, ran a much greater risk of death from exposure than their more hardy British-born colleagues.

The recession in Britain in the thirties had hit the shipbuilding industry hard, cutting back both the nation's share of the world market and the number of new vessels being produced in the shipyards. When the war started, in fact, there were actually 2,000 fewer merchant ships at sea than had been operated at the end of the First World War. And the remaining ships had to cater for a population that had increased by four million.

To maximise the shipping available, the Admiralty set up a Trade Division in Whitehall to plan the routing of British merchant ships in conjunction with naval control officers located in ports all over the world. Churchill, who took a keen personal interest in the operation, also authorised generous insurance cover to shipowners to ensure that every vessel capable of carrying cargo was put to sea.

A predictable result of this largesse was that many vessels that would in other times have gone to the knacker's yard were prepared for sea once again. Stories are told of some owners seizing the opportunity to make a quick profit by firing up ancient ships that had been lying rusting in docks and on rivers for years. When these boats were taken over by their new crews, the encrusted dirt and swarms of insects that had long lived undisturbed combined to make the conditions almost unbearable.

The need to expand the merchant service – and keep pace with the high loss of ships and crew – resulted in a lot of young men going to sea for the first time. Those who volunteered were immediately exempted from call-up into the armed services. Many of them – men like Paddy Mulholland – were undoubtedly attracted by the sense of adventure the sea offered as well as by freedom from the kind of discipline inherent in the armed forces. The dangers of U-boats, torpedoes and mines were rarely discussed and any training these new recruits received before joining a ship was rudimentary at best.

For quite a few of the raw recruits, the reality of their situation was not long in being brought home to them as Dönitz's *Rudeltaktiks* continued to blow vessels from the ocean. In December 1939, Churchill was informed that a total of 150 merchant ships had been lost during the year – half a million tons of vessels, which amounted to over two per cent of the merchant navy's pre-war strength.

One consequence of the U-boats' success in savaging the supply lines was that reserves of raw materials including oil and iron ore fell dramatically and restrictions had to be put on food in January 1940. Certain products including bacon, ham, eggs, butter and sugar, were rationed to four ounces per adult per week, making life increasingly hard for the British housewife with a young family.

The chill of apprehension that had settled across Britain that winter was made worse by the arctic weather conditions that gripped the country during the first months of 1940. The Germans took advantage of the situation to carry out extensive mine-laying operations around the east coast and this, combined with U-boat activities in the North Sea and the Atlantic, resulted in another one hundred merchant ships being destroyed by mid-February. By contrast, the best efforts of the British convoy escorts and mine layers had managed to destroy only about a dozen of the German submarines.

May 1940 saw a crisis in Parliament about the government's handling of the war and the resignation of the prime minister, Neville Chamberlain. On 10 May, he was replaced by Winston Churchill. The former head of the Admiralty wasted no time in forming a coalition government of all the parties. Five days later, however, he received the grim news that the German Army had occupied Holland, Belgium and France. The enemy would soon be on the doorstep, he realised.

With all his other preoccupations, Churchill still insisted that every possible effort must be used to maintain the flow of merchant shipping between Britain and America. Privately, he talked to his friend Roosevelt in the White House and appealed for the loan of some older destroyers and aircraft for use on escort duties. Once again, Churchill reiterated his conviction that Hitler was probably already nursing ideas about installing a Nazi government in the USA one day...

The evidence that 43 U-boats were now known to be operational only underlined the prime minister's fears. Indeed, unbeknown to him, on 24 May Dönitz had ordered unrestricted attacks by his *Rudeltaktik* on all merchant shipping in the Atlantic, stressing that complete destruction of the ships was imperative. Before the end of that month a grisly tally showed that over 60,000 tons of merchant shipping had gone to the bottom of the ocean.

In June, Britain was all alone in Europe after the retreat from Dunkirk and now almost wholly dependent on supplies from across the Atlantic. During the month the cost of this vital link was a record total of 289,000 tons of shipping lost to the U-boats – amounting to one ship sunk every 24 hours.

The summer of 1940 also saw the arrival of another threat to British merchant shipping – the 'Ghost Cruisers', converted

German merchant ships that carried batteries of guns and torpedo tubes concealed behind dummy funnels and deck housing. These 7,000-ton vessels capable of long voyages looked for all the world like any other peaceful merchantman – until an unfortunate British vessel allowed one to get too close.

The free reign the U-boat commanders had been given to hunt down and destroy any merchantman caused the subsequent few months to be referred to by the submariners as the 'happy time.' Between July and October, 217 vessels representing over a million tons of merchant shipping went to the bottom of the Atlantic. Dönitz, for his part, lost just two U-boats.

Even while other members of Hitler's staff talked up an invasion of England, the Führer himself remained convinced that by cutting off supply routes from America he could ultimately force Britain give up what he now believed to be an unequal struggle. Nazi propaganda also swung into full cry to publicise the feats of its submarine captains and their men, often ridiculously exaggerating what were in any event very substantial losses of British ships. And all the time, Dönitz continued to urge his men, 'What we sink today is what matters more than anything we sink in two or three years' time.'

The mass destruction of British merchant shipping by the U-boats continued throughout the winter of 1940 with small convoys of merchantmen regularly being surrounded by packs of the submarines and obliterated. By the end of the year, the Admiralty estimated that 4 million tons of shipping had been destroyed and 5,622 merchant seaman had died among the total of 23,922 forced to abandon their ships. Three million tons *less* of cargo was now being carried than at the start of the year with a meagre one million tons of new shipping being put to sea during the same period.

It took great resolve on the part of the increasingly weary merchant seamen to return to their ships after each crossing of the Atlantic. The ever-present threat of the U-boats, the occasional sightings and (if they were lucky) the narrow misses, played havoc with even the most experienced sailor's nerves. During that spring, real fears began to be voiced that it might soon be difficult to crew the vessels, such was the level of casualties and, even more ominously, the number of men threatening not to sign on or simply deserting their ships.

Fate – in the person of the American president, Franklin Roosevelt – came to the aid of the nation and his friend, Winston Churchill, in March 1941. The prime minister, ever the optimist, had already stated that his primary objective in 1941 was to build up 'such a supply of weapons both by increased output at home and through ocean-borne supplies, as will lay the foundation of victory'. He estimated that at least 3 million tons of additional merchant shipping capacity would be essential to this objective and only the US was capable of filling the requirement. In what he later described as 'one of the most important letters I ever wrote,' the prime minister appealed to Roosevelt:

The more rapid and abundant flow of munitions and ships which you are able to send us, the sooner will our dollar credits be exhausted. The moment approaches when we shall no longer be able to pay cash for shipping and other supplies. While we will do our utmost and shrink from no proper sacrifice to make payments across the exchange, I believe that you will agree it would be wrong in principle and mutually disadvantage us if, at the height of this struggle, Great Britain were to be divested of all saleable assets so that after victory was won with our blood, civilisation saved and time gained for the United States to be fully armed against all eventualities, we should stand stripped to the bone.

The effect of this emotional letter on Franklin Roosevelt was evidently profound. After pondering on Churchill's words and their inference, he had the flash of inspiration that would result in the creation of the famous 'Lend-Lease Agreement'. Later, in a press conference held at the White House, he explained to reporters:

> In all history, no major war has ever been lost through lack of money. Now what I want to do is to eliminate the dollar sign. That is something brand new in the thoughts of everybody in this room, I think – get rid of the silly, foolish old dollar sign.

What Roosevelt proposed was that American industry, instead of fulfilling British contracts on an ad hoc basis, would now have its output centrally contracted and controlled by the government, which would determine whether armaments were to be used by the US forces or allocated to others 'fighting in the common defence of democracy'. American aircraft, tanks and especially shipping would be made available on request to such defenders of freedom, he said. And in a radio broadcast to the entire American people, the president spelt out the implications of his scheme:

> If Britain should go down, all of us in America would be living at the point of a gun. A gun loaded with explosive bullets, economic as well as military. We must produce arms and ships with every energy and resource we can command. We must be the great Arsenal of Democracy.'

On 11 March, the Lease-Lend Bill, coded, appropriately, HR 1776, was signed by Roosevelt after being passed by both Houses of Congress. The White House lawyers had even found a precedent supporting Roosevelt's bill – an almost forgotten statute of 1892 that allowed the Secretary of War 'to lease military property when it will be for the public good'.

Although there were still those isolationist members of Congress who were not happy to be involved in what they regarded as a strictly European quarrel, Roosevelt had his way and took the step that wedded the United States to the British fight against Nazism and that would, ultimately, lead to the country entering the Second World War.

While these delicate negotiations had been going on, however, the U-boats had continued ravaging British merchant shipping. Hitler had also added his voice to that of Dönitz by urging that his forces 'concentrate every means of waging war by sea and air on enemy supplies'.

As spring turned into summer, Winston Churchill was given the alarming news that he was loosing ships at the rate of over 7 million tons a year, which was three times as fast as the shipyards could build replacements. To make matters worse, some two and a half million tons of ships were either out of action undergoing repairs or else being refurbished while they were actually being loaded. As a direct result, the imports of raw materials and food had fallen by nearly a fifth and officials began seriously to worry whether the war economy could be sustained through to 1942, let alone beyond that date.

Ration books now became an everyday fact of life in Britain and the rationing of food, which had been introduced in January 1940, was tightened still further. Meat, eggs and cheese were in very short supply and when tea, too, had to be rationed, the men and women in the streets of the nation knew things were bad. But the 'Siege of Britain' – as it became known – did nothing to dampen the spirits or determination of the people, as exemplified by Churchill himself. And when the first cargoes of American food arrived in May under the new Lend-Lease Agreement, there was even room for smiles as some 6 million eggs were distributed to the nation's housewives.

The prime minister also seized this moment to announce formally what he termed 'The Battle of the Atlantic' in a directive that stated: 'The next four months should enable us to defeat the attempt to strangle our food supplies and our connections with the United States. For this purpose we must take the offensive against the U-boats.

A top-level Battle of Atlantic Committee was set up and one of its first actions was to try to get the damaged merchant ships moving more quickly from the shipyards where they were awaiting repairs by releasing 40,000 men from the armed forces to work in the docks. The number of destroyers escorting the convoys was also increased and the Navy's anti-submarine tactics were changed to emphasise team work: they were to share information about the enemy's whereabouts and attack in clusters.

When a pair of U-boats were destroyed in a single engagement using these new techniques there was cause for a little optimism. But, by the end of April 1941, another quarter of a million tons of merchant shipping had been sunk as Dönitz's submarines ranged ever further, going even to the coast of Iceland. Here they had the pick of slower-moving vessels, which had deliberately been routed further north.

The Atlantic Committee realised that an increase in the materials being provided under the Lend-Lease Agreement was now essential. In response to another appeal from Churchill for more aid – including aircraft, ammunition, food and ships – Roosevelt agreed to help and sent a message to the British prime minister that must have really warmed his heart: 'Arrangements will be made to repair British merchant ships and warships in US dockyards. I have allotted funds for the building of 58 additional shipping ways and 200 additional ships.' The only proviso the president made was that the British *must* crew and sail all of these vessels with their own people.

Tom Watson, a young Glaswegian merchant seaman whose ship, the *Clydebank*, was among the first vessels to benefit from this policy in the summer of 1941, was already a veteran of the Atlantic crossings. He later recalled how he had become involved in these crucial events:

> As soon as the war was declared, I applied for a job on this armed merchant ship. I didn't fancy the army and, anyhow, my da had been a seaman. I was only just eighteen and I remember this old sailor who lived near me who said, 'Don't go on one of those ships – they are death traps.
>
> But I still signed on for two years and my pay was £2 a week. They gave us two weeks' pay in advance and I went home to Bridgeton and spent the lot on drink before I joined my ship. The old man was right, though, I did risk my life with those U-boats every time we crossed the Atlantic.

Tom also remembered how desperate the merchant navy was at that time for crew members. Before sailing on another trip to the US in September 1941, he heard the first rumours that even prisoners just released from Barlinnie were being recruited. The story particularly stuck in his mind because some of the men were said to be 'real head-cases' who belonged to the most violent gangs in his own district of Bridgeton.

And it is thanks to Tom Watson's knowledge of this part of Glasgow and its turbulent history that we have an insider's view of the gangster culture to which those men who went to sea at a crucial moment in the Battle of the Atlantic belonged.

Chapter 3

At War with the 'Neds'

Bridgeton, which was the home patch of the Billy Boys and the Norman Conks, two of the most notorious gangs in Glasgow in the 1930s, had once been one of the prettiest of the ten villages that formed that part of the city north of the Clyde. Built on lands known as 'Barrowfield', which are mentioned in records as far back as the sixteenth century, the character of the locality had changed rapidly into that of an industrial community after the building of the Rutherglen Bridge over the Clyde in 1776. A new road running north from the bridge became known as Main Street, Bridgeton, and after this streets and houses were laid out in the kind of regular grid pattern which would be immediately familiar to any American visitor.

It was the construction of a dye-works just to the east of the Rutherglen Bridge in 1785 that accelerated the transition. To accommodate the workforce required by the company for its calico printing, houses were built and the roads on which they stood were named after famous inventors and reformers such as Franklin, Rumford and Colbert. Less distinguished in name, but more notorious, Norman Street, not far from the bridge and Abercromby Street off the London Road, came into being some time later.

By the early years of the nineteenth century, the green fields of the district had increasingly given way to cotton spinning and weaving mills while at the same time the population grew rapidly. Factories soon encircled Bridgeton, and their workers and their families were forced into crowded, insanitary 'back lands', as a local clergyman, Reverend Logan Aikman, wrote in 1875:

At this date, the population of the district has reached 64,000; and its crowded factories and workshops of all kinds may be counted by scores, covering acres of what, a few years ago, were waving corn fields, and pouring forth, through forests of tall, grimy, furnace stalks, at all hours of the day, volumes of dense black smoke, giving the district now very much the appearance of the chimney-top of the neighbouring city.

The sprawling size of the industries operating in Bridgeton, which included engineering, ironfounding, chemical works, pottery, carpet weaving and brewing, soon caused it to be absorbed into the greater mass of Glasgow. Reports about the factories at this time indicate that many of the men and women worked in cramped and unhealthy conditions and children as young as nine were also being employed in several of the spinning mills. Most of these people lived in two-room apartments on a diet largely consisting of porridge, potatoes and sour milk.

A bread riot and a typhus epidemic did nothing to enhance the reputation of Bridgeton during the latter part of the nineteenth century. For many inhabitants drink became one escape from their 'reeky and noisome haunts', and it was not unusual on Sunday mornings to see fifty or so drunks asleep on Glasgow Green. Vice, gambling and sport were other diversions, with football enthusiastically played by many of the young men in matches so fiercely contested that they often ended in violence. (Interestingly, it was on Glasgow Green that a football club that later became one of the most famous in Scotland, Glasgow Rangers, was formed in 1873 by a group of keen *rowers* led by three brothers named McNeil.)

The decline of the condition of the tenements in roads such as Abercromby Street and Norman Street continued into the twentieth century and the dissatisfaction with their lot, coupled to a lack of employment caused by the increasing mechanisation of industry, bred young men and women who turned easily to dissipation, violence and crime. For the young males particularly, joining a local gang was the only way of achieving any kind of status.

In the thirties, Bridgeton was home to several gangs, including the Bluebells, who specialised in disrupting dance halls; the Nunnies from Nuneaton Street; and the Baltic Fleet, a group of young tearaways who had used rhyming slang to adapt the name of their home territory in Baltic Street, so called because of the Baltic Jute Company that was briefly based there.

But all of these mobs paled in comparison with the Billy Boys and Norman Conks, described by the social historian, A. W. Cockerill, writing a few years later, as 'two of the most vicious and mercurial gangs ever to flow through the streets of Glasgow'.

Glasgow police records indicate that the first gangs of anti-social young men were reported in the city's streets in the 1880s. Originally they were known as 'Keelies', but by the close of the century the expression had been changed to the 'Neds' – a term that the police, the public and even the young men themselves used.

The first organised gang appears to have been the 'Penny Mob', so named because this was the weekly levy imposed on all members, whose numbers ran into hundreds. According to newspaper accounts of the time, the money was collected so that when one of the mob was arrested and brought before a court, the funds could be used to pay his fine.

The young gang members were a mixture of violent and dangerous thugs and weak-willed and not very intelligent followers-on. Some were unemployed (probably unemployable), while others had drifted into the gangs because of their upbringing and poverty. They exerted their authority over one another – and their streets – with fists, bottles and an incredible variety of knives.

As the new century dawned, however, the numbers of gangs increased rapidly, and their developing organisational skills proved a threat that was difficult for the police to keep under control. They were now identified by curious names or the parts of Glasgow from which they came: the Hi Hi from the north end; the Ping Pong gang from the east side; and several from the southern areas including the South Side Stickers, the Village Boys and the Tim Malloy gang.

In the immediate aftermath of the First World War, two Glasgow mobs regularly fought for supremacy: the Black Hand gang and the Redskins. Some unfortunate city officials tried to dismiss them on the basis of their 'childish' names as being just groups of unemployed youths who had lived through the violence and bloodshed of the war without being old enough to take part and now wanted to generate their own type of excitement. The Glasgow writer, Clifford Hanley, who lived through this era, wrote in his autobiography, *Dancing in the Streets* (1958):

> Glasgow, in spite of its sooty grey look, or maybe because of it, has always needed colour and the gangs gave colour to some people, if it was only the colour of blood. These were never comparable to the Prohibition gangs of Chicago. The American gangs were illegal business enterprises that used violence and death as trading methods in the rational

50

pursuit of profit. Glasgow gangs never made any money for anybody. Gang bosses never graduated to Cadillacs or even Austin Sevens, far less villas on the coast and political pull. They just wanted to fight. They started poor and they finished poor and they stayed poor in between.

In truth, though, there were also a number of well-known villains in both the Black Hand gang and the Redskins who used their experience, and the hedonism of the younger hooligans, to orchestrate crimes of robbery, theft and violence. Typical of these was Aggie Reid of the Redskins who was feared for his skill with a cut-throat razor which he used either as a threat to all and sundry or else to demand protection money from local shopkeepers.

By 1924, the Beehive Gang and its leader Peter Williamson were also a force to be reckoned with by other gangs and the police. Williamson, a tall, powerfully built man in his early twenties who was said to have come from a respectable background, masterminded his gang in housebreaking, robberies, intimidations and the occasional mob attack. Quick-witted and a dangerous man with his fists, he avoided arrest on numerous occasions. For a time there were said to be few other criminals in Glasgow able to hold their own against Williamson.

Fights among the gangs were frequent, injuries regular, but actual deaths rare. One much-publicised killing occurred in March 1924 when a fight broke out at the Bedford Parlour Dance Hall in Celtic Street between the Parlour Boys and another mob, the Bridgegate Boys from Gallowgate, who had ill-advisedly entered the hall to escape a torrential downpour. When the two sets of rivals saw each other, a pitched battle broke out during which one of the Parlour Boys, James 'Razzle-Dazzle' Dalziel (so named because of his love of loud clothing) was fatally stabbed in the throat.

51

Although one of the Bridgegate gang, William Collins, was subsequently arrested and charged with murder, when he and several others who had been involved in the affray were bought before the Glasgow Sheriff Court, the jury were unable to agree that Collins had struck the death blow. According to a report of the case, he was sent down smirking and gesticulating at his admirers to serve a sentence of just 12 months.

By the late twenties, two gangs had become particularly feared throughout Glasgow and constantly vied for supremacy on their home patch of Bridgeton. They were the Billy Boys from Abercromby Street adjacent to the Calton Burying Ground and the Norman Conquerors from Norman Street, known more familiarly as the Norman Conks. The roots of both gangs lay in sectarian differences and a love of drink, sex, violence and crime.

More than one commentator on sectarian violence has observed that Glasgow's militant Catholics and Protestants took their aggressive inspiration from Ireland. The Billy Boys came from a predominantly Protestant neighbourhood and their name was inspired by Prince William of Orange, while the Norman Conks were Catholics. Both utilised traditional dates like the Twelfth of July – the day of the Orange Walk – as an excuse for intimidation, fighting and a chance to settle old scores.

Although the history of both gangs is difficult to detail accurately, the Billy Boys were believed to have been the older of the two rival factions. There are reports of occasional fights between them and another bunch of hooligans, the Sally Boys – named after their home patch, Salamanca Street – in the twenties, which ended in court appearances for the main culprits.

By the mid-1920s, the gang was led by Billy Fullerton – fêted in local legend as 'King Billy', a man noted for his recklessness and love of a fight. Said to be a natural leader, he instituted a system for attacking other hoodlums after they had collected their *buroo* [protection money] from shopkeepers and using it to pay the fines of his members. Occasionally, he would send groups of his followers to put the frighteners on shopkeepers themselves.

Fullerton's rise to prominence came in the wake of a football match played on Glasgow Green in 1924. The game was supposed to have been a 'friendly' between the Billy Boys and the Kent Star, a Catholic gang from nearby Calton. But after Fullerton had scored the winning goal, he was attacked and beaten with a hammer by the disgruntled losers. After his recovery, the enraged Fullerton raised a gang of several hundred young thugs and they exacted a terrible revenge on the Kent Star men in Calton. Thereafter he was usually to be found in Gilmour's Club in Olympia Street by Bridgeton Cross ostensibly acting as a bouncer but actually holding court, surrounded by his acolytes. He would encourage his followers to shout the provocative words, 'God save the King!' at any suspected Catholic hoodlum who passed by.

No one appears seriously to have challenged the Billy Boys' supremacy until the emergence of the Norman Conks across the other side of the district near the Rutherglen Bridge. Their leader was 'Bull' Bowman, a vicious young man in the same mould as Fullerton who favoured the use of pickshafts – pieces of hardwood measuring 42 inches in length and weighing nearly three pounds – when he and his followers laid into their enemies.

Apart from the occasional skirmishes when small groups of gang members came across each other at dance halls and cinemas, there were also specific occasions when the Billy Boys and the Norman Conks set out to challenge one another. A regular confrontation took place on Sunday mornings, when the Billy Boys would mass and march up Poplin Street and down French Street, which lay at either end of Norman

Street, singing one particular song to the tune of 'Marching Through Georgia':

Hullo! Hullo! We are the Billy Boys.
Hullo! Hullo! We are the Billy Boys.
Up tae the knees in Fenian blood, surrender or ye'll die
For we are the Bridgeton Billy Boys.

Unless the Norman Conks were feeling particularly incensed and suitably prepared for a battle, they would normally content themselves with hurling abuse in return. On saints' days and holy days, however, the Billy Boys would attempt to turn into Norman Street *itself* and then all hell would break loose.

This diversion was typical of the reckless leadership of William Fullerton. He usually left robbery and suchlike to other members of the gang, but he was always close to the front of the procession and would shout the first challenge at the faces pressed against the windows of the tenements. At this, bottles, bricks and pickshafts would be hurled in all directions.

'Bull' Bowman could be equally aggressive when looking for a *shellacking*. On one famous occasion, he and some three hundred members of the Norman Conks armed with pickshafts attached themselves to a protest march organised by the National Unemployed Workers' Movement. Bowman, of course, knew that the protesters' route would take them through Abercomby Street, and once the road was reached, a pitched battle broke out which resulted in considerable damage to property and injury to several policemen called to the scene who tried in vain to keep the warring factions apart. The advantage of surprise resulted in a notable victory for the Conks.

Among the weapons used by both gangs were bottles, hatchets, swords, sharpened bicycle chains and, occasionally, guns, knives and razors. Beer bottles were one of the favourite implements as they could be carried quite legitimately, while it was unwise to be caught in possession of a gun or knife. A bottle could also be used as a club to knock a man down before kicking him in the face; or, alternatively, when smashed, the jagged edges would cause terrible injuries to an adversary.

Whenever fights were being specifically planned in the vicinity of either Abercomby Street or Norman Street, weapons were often carried there by the gang members' girlfriends – known either as 'queens' or 'bits of stuff' – concealed in their clothes. This was a foolproof ploy as the girls (and their menfolk) knew only too well that no police officer would dare search a female for fear of being accused of assaulting her.

As the thirties dawned, it was evident that the Glasgow police were losing the battle to curtail the 'Neds' in Bridgeton and the other parts of the city where they held sway. The gangsters had become expert at fading into the darkness or the impenetrable tenement blocks whenever the 'busies' arrived. Even those men who were stopped and questioned had no trouble in finding others who would provide them with alibis. Only those hooligans knocked insensible or injured so seriously that they had to go to the Royal Infirmary were in any danger of finding themselves on a charge or in court.

There could be no doubt in anyone's mind, then, that a situation existed in which crime threatened to swamp the law in Glasgow. A remarkable man was required to redress the balance – and into this ferment came an imposing figure with the curious name of Percy Sillitoe, a former colonial law-officer now turned crime fighter in Scotland.

Sir Percy Joseph Sillitoe is probably best remembered today as the former director general of MI5 and the inspiration for one of Ian Fleming's James Bond novels, *Diamonds Are Forever* (1956). The two men had become friends during their careers in Britain's counter-espionage service, and Sillitoe's involvement in solving the case of the Rand diamond-smuggling ring gave Fleming the idea for one of the best adventures of his legendary spy.

In fact, much earlier than this, Sillitoe had been a dedicated police officer in South Africa and then a successful gangster-fighting chief constable in Sheffield, before fate took him to Glasgow. Later, in 1942, when he was appointed chief constable of Kent as the fear of German invasion threatened that coast, he became the first chief constable who had worked in Scotland to be knighted. The facts about the man and his career serve to illustrate *why* he most probably condoned the press-ganging of criminals into merchant seamen for the jail that went to sea.

Percy Sillitoe was born in Tulse Hill, South London, and as a child was often teased about his name – a fact for which he was later grateful, 'because it taught me to control my temper and sit stoically and with an appearance of unconcern in the face of taunts and mockery.' The man destined to become a key upholder of the law, once jokingly suggested the family might have been descended from the law-breaking Vandal, Stilicho, who nearly seized the Roman Empire.

Joseph Sillitoe, Percy's father, was an inveterate gambler and philanderer who lost his inheritance in a series of disastrous investments and is reputed to have ended his days in a workhouse after being in and out of jail on vagrancy charges. Percy rarely talked about him, yet was devoted to his mother and later regularly sent money for her upkeep.

Percy's mother passed on to him her love of music, and his singing voice gained him a place at the St Paul's Cathedral Choir School in 1898, where he trained for four years. Here he is said to have developed the strong sense of self-discipline that became a hallmark of his life and career. At fourteen, however, the young chorister who was rapidly growing into a tall, handsome man with a jutting chin and intense blue eyes, found that his voice had broken and he had to abandon any idea of a singing career.

In 1908, for reasons that have never been fully explained, though he may well have been influenced by a revulsion at what had become of his father, Percy Sillitoe decided to enlist in the British South Africa Police in Rhodesia. In the years that followed, he learned the art of detection in the wild, hardened himself as a rider and a boxer, narrowly missed being savaged by a lion, and whenever he was engaged on a manhunt doggedly adhered to the maxim, 'Never come back without your man'.

During this period of his life when promotions and fresh postings took him to what are now Tanzania and Zambia, Sillitoe honed the skills that would make him such a good policeman and spy catcher. He also became an expert big-game hunter and a fine shot, revealing a calculating efficiency with a gun. Living in Africa, however, played havoc with his health and after a particularly virulent bout of rheumatic fever, he decided to return to England in 1922.

Thanks to some help from a relative and the undoubted value of his experiences in South Africa, Sillitoe was able to secure the position of chief constable of Chesterfield. He immediately set about changing the traditional role of the chief constable and realigning the role of his officers in a society radically changed by the First World War. He also won the support of these men by demolishing the force's cramped old headquarters and constructing new, more accommodating buildings.

Sillitoe was, however, soon restless for new challenges and in 1924 moved on to become chief constable of the East Riding of Yorkshire. Here, again, he was at the forefront of improving methods of policing and raising the morale of his men, although he found the general run-of-the-mill-work dealing with the 'odd drunk, the occasional poacher and sometimes a truculent country squire treating police constables like servants' did not really challenge him. After just fourteen months, he moved again to Sheffield and the real mettle of the man was tested.

It took only a matter of days after taking office in May 1926 for Sillitoe to realise that the city was in the grip of gang warfare, which the police seemed powerless to stop. As one local reporter put it at the time, 'Sheffield was rapidly becoming a little Chicago – for many people the law was that of the jungle: the strong rule and the weak give in.'

Intimidation of local shopkeepers by the gangsters was rife and the public were victims of constant robbery and theft, frequently carried out with considerable violence. Sillitoe soon discovered that two gangs, one led by George Mooney and the other by Sam Garvin, were the main culprits and, between them, had gained virtual control of the poorer areas of Sheffield, in particular the drab back streets of the Park district and the Crofts and Norfolk Bridge areas. As Sillitoe later confided in his autobiography, *Cloak Without Dagger* (1955):

In 1926, these three districts were, without any doubt, as rough and lawless as any to be found in England. The publicans and shopkeepers lived in daily terror of the Mooney and Garvin gangs for, when they were not gambling or thieving or fighting among themselves – one of their favourite pastimes was robbing public houses. They would order whiskies and cigarettes, drain their glasses, pocket their cigarettes and announce, 'We're the Mooney Boys' and leave. No one dared challenge them to pay and it was clear that neither they or the Garvin boys were afraid of the police.

Local officers for their part were afraid of being beaten and disfigured if they tried to arrest any of the gangsters, and members of the public were unwilling to give evidence in the magistrates' courts for fear of retaliation. Sillitoe decided to confront the problem by meeting force with greater force and hand-picking the biggest and toughest officers from among his 700 policemen to form a special 'flying squad'.

Such methods would, of course, not be tolerated today, but Sillitoe was a believer in taking drastic action to meet what he saw as a crisis situation and was fully prepared to risk incurring public censure. He knew that complaints of police brutality would in all probability arise from certain quarters, but was convinced he would have the support of all the decent, law-abiding citizens of Sheffield.

Among the batch of robust officers pleased to have the opportunity of taking on the hoodlums at their own game was Sergeant Joseph Robinson. He believed that Sillitoe's predecessors had been too tolerant – perhaps even scared – of the cloth-capped villains and he had already taken on occasions to handing out his own brand of justice. Small wonder, then, that when Robinson heard the new chief's plan he embraced the idea enthusiastically.

Sillitoe's instructions to his men were quite simple: 'Hit first and ask questions afterwards.' The policemen were given an intensive course in street fighting, trained in ju-jitsu and rough-housing, and then sent out in pairs in plain clothes to take on the 'cowardly little gangster rats' – as one officer referred to them – on their own territory. All were fired up with enthusiasm for their task by the chief they had now nick-named 'the Captain'.

Sergeant Robinson, carrying only a short wooden staff known as a 'detective baton' under his plain clothes, was to recall later in an interview with the *Sheffield Telegraph* that early skirmishes between the 'flying squad' and the armed gangsters put members of both sides in hospital. After one particularly brutal confrontation in the Park district, he had to help a colleague to hospital for medical attention to seventeen stab wounds.

But the no-nonsense attitude of the gang-busters gradually gained the respect of the public as Sillitoe had hoped and also began to worry all but the most hardened criminals. Robinson told the *Telegraph* that one of his most cherished memories had been when he and three colleagues, 'as good as challenged one of the mobs':

We heard that they were planning to get us because we had turned them out of a pub the night before. I decided not to wait for them to come to us and I took three of my men, Geraghty, Loxley and Lunn, to a pub in West Bar. Sure enough they were there, about a dozen of them. I knew we would be in trouble, so I told them I was going to search them. We found razors and coshes on them, but they knew we were out to settle it once and for all.

Then the fun started. It was quite a set-to and I shall never forget it. It was the only way to settle them, and we three showed the twelve of them what for. That's how we stopped it. We kept after them all the time. I told them that three or more was a crowd and I wouldn't let them get together in bars. If I found them together my boys would split them up. We harried them until we wore them down.

The 'flying squad' were soon filling the Sheffield courts with gangsters caught in the act of violence or robbery, the razors, knives and coshes taken from them by the police laid out before the bench in mute but incriminating evidence against them. Sillitoe himself was often present at these trials supporting the actions of his officers and re-emphasising his determination to drive crime from the streets of Sheffield.

Those citizens who had thought the tall, well-spoken and courteous man might be no match for the hardmen of the city soon learned that he had an iron fist in his velvet glove. Within two years, Sillitoe was being hailed throughout Yorkshire as 'The Gang Buster of Sheffield' and in an interview in the *Yorkshire Telegraph and Star* he explained his philosophy in the simplest and most direct terms:

> I believe that there is only one way to deal with the gangster mentality. You must show that you are not afraid. If you stand up to them and they realise that you mean business, they will soon knuckle under. The element of beast in man, whether it comes from an unhappy and impoverished background, or from his own undisciplined lustful appetites, will respond exactly as a wild beast in the jungle responds – to nothing but greater force and greater firmness of purpose.

Sergeant Robinson, whom Sillitoe also publicly praised for his efforts, was quick to return the compliment. 'He was a damn fine chief, was "the Captain", and there is no doubt about that.' The mutual respect the two had for each other would, of course, see them reunited when Sillitoe moved on to his next position.

The campaign against the gangsters netted its biggest fish after a clash between the Mooney and Garvin gangs when the two top men were arrested and sentenced to prison. After George Mooney was released from jail, Sillitoe had him brought to his office and warned him that if he or Garvin continued their evil ways, he would crush them both out of existence. The chief constable went on to tell the surprised gangster that he believed he had some good in him and should try to better himself. The policeman then offered his hand:

> I shall never forget the sight of George Mooney, gang leader of such terrifying reputation, grasping my hand as his face

worked like an emotional child's. Happily he became – and remained – one of Sheffield's respectable citizens.

This memory stayed with Sillitoe as he continued to modernise the Sheffield police force – introducing a forensic laboratory and police boxes, and recruiting additional women police officers – until, in 1931, he was offered an even bigger challenge further north in the city of Glasgow.

Sillitoe's reputation as 'THE MAN WHO SMASHED THE RAZOR GANGS' – to quote another Sheffield newspaper headline – preceeded him to Glasgow, the 'Second City of the Empire', where he arrived in late November 1931. The members of the Billy Boys and the Norman Conks probably smiled at the thought of this *bam-pot* copper being sent to try to put them down and ordered another round of drinks in their respective Bridgeton pubs. The Sheffield gangs may have caved in to him, but they reckoned they were a much tougher bunch.

The appointment of 'the Captain' was not, though, universally popular. Although the situation clearly demanded someone with his experience to combat the gangsters terrorising the city of over one million people, there were questions being asked in the press about whether that man should be 'from south of the border'.

Once again Sillitoe had to set out to win over the doubters and alert his force of 2,500 men – the second-largest in the UK – that he was a man with a mission. Once more, too, he had to raise morale, offering the younger men the chance of promotion while gently removing some of the more senior officers long past pensionable age and too set in their ways.

When the new chief constable had had a chance to study the appalling crime figures attributed to the gangster elements of the city, he wasted no time in deciding to send for Sergeant Robinson to head up a new gang-busting 'flying squad'. And with the savings he knew he could achieve from staff and cost cutting, Sillitoe was able to make available money to spend on erecting police boxes at strategic points across the city and putting fast, radio patrol cars on the streets – a pioneer idea he picked up from a police convention in the 'gangster capital', Chicago.

Sillitoe also started to involve himself in the life of the city, showing concern for the underprivileged, the unemployed and the ordinary, decent citizens trying to make the best of their lives in a place beset by vice, corruption and graft as well as divided by sectarian rivalry. With his strong humanitarian leanings, he also found time to assist the protesters in the Great Hunger March, organise an annual outing for poor children, and make visits to Barlinnie Jail where he helped in the rehabilitation of prisoners by organising lectures and sporting matches with other prisons, and providing help, food and clothes for the destitute families of some inmates.

But it was getting to grips with the gangster problem that really drove Chief Constable Sillitoe, as he later wrote in *Cloak Without Dagger*:

> When I arrived in Glasgow, two of the most notorious gangs were the Norman Conquerors and the Billy Boys who were, of course, bitter enemies, and frequently provoked each other resulting in much injury. But I deeply resented that my police officers should be constantly involved in these loutish riots in the course of which they were attacked by both sides at once.

First, Sillitoe made a study of the gangsters, how they were organised and what crimes they committed, gathering huge files of reports of their crimes and pitched battles. From this it became evident that the Glasgow 'Neds' were much more numerous and violent than the thugs he had dealt with in

63

Sheffield. So, with the aid of the redoubtable Sergeant Robinson, he devised a systematic battle plan to put the gangs out of business. He gave a clear warning of his intentions to the public at large in a statement to the *Glasgow Sunday Mail* early in 1934:

We are determined to fight the city gangsters with the utmost ferocity. These hooligans are mostly unemployable louts from the slum districts whose education and environment have given them a complete contempt for the law. They are craven-hearted rats when alone. They find their courage in numbers and they fight with iron bars and knives and with their boots. We are out to teach them that they must take heed of the law.

The statement must have sounded like a call to arms to the Billy Boys and Norman Conks and it is a fact that crime actually rose in Glasgow that year – the number of property crimes, for instance, showed an increase from 7,626 to 13,539. But Sergeant Robinson and his men were already beginning to make their presence felt, especially in Bridgeton where they made a point of turning up regularly at the Bridgeton Cross to hassle the gangsters hanging around there waiting for something to happen.

Indeed, whenever William Fullerton or 'Bull' Bowman decided to send their men to break into houses, carry out smash-and-grab raids, or intimidate shopkeepers, watching eyes were never far away. The new police boxes and radio cars were also soon in operation helping to keep track of the gangsters' whereabouts and, if necessary, dispatching officers to the scene. Sillitoe even managed to recruit a number of 'grasses' among the gangsters themselves to help him gather information; one notable recruit was Aggie Reid whose Redskins had now dispersed.

'The Jail That Went To Sea,' the *George Washington* in New York harbour.

ABOVE: To combat the menace of German U-Boats, many merchant ships were armed with 12-pound guns left over from World War One.

RIGHT: One of the earliest accounts of the Merchant Navy's part in the Battle of the Atlantic, published in 1941.

THE MERCHANT NAVY

FIGHTS

TRAMPS AGAINST U-BOATS

BY A.D. DIVINE

HELP WIN THE WAR ON THE KITCHEN FRONT

 MINISTRY OF FOOD

BULLETIN No. 3   June, 1940

We should use less tea. If each

of us gives up one teaspoonful in

every four, we shall save shipping

space for 50,000 tons of war

material in a year. This is a

war contribution which one and all

should make.

                    THE MINISTER OF FOOD

ABOVE ALL AVOID WASTE AND SO SAVE SHIPPING

ABOVE: Percy Sillitoe, the Glasgow Crime-Buster, whose officers helped in the 'recruitment' of men for the *George Washington*.

LEFT: A typical Government advertisement urging British housewives to help the cause of the beleaguered Merchant Navy.

A back-street of the Bridgeton slums in Glasgow during the Thirties.

LEFT: Captain David Bone, the veteran merchant seaman, assigned to captain the *George Washington*.

CENTRE: The *Cameronia*, Captain David Bone's first command, that was torpedoed and sunk in the Mediterranean in 1917.

BELOW: The *Pasteur*, which carried a number of the Scottish ex-convicts across the Atlantic.

ABOVE: The *Llangibby Castle*, another of the ships used to convey the mixed bag of seamen to America to crew the *George Washington*.

BELOW: League Island Navy Yard in Philadelphia, where the crew of the *George Washington* first set eyes on their ship.

ABOVE: Following the Japanese attack on Pearl Harbour, League Island became jammed with vessels hastily being made seaworthy.

BELOW: Ready to sail, the *George Washington* in Philadelphia in January 1942.

The *George Washington* at sea – one of the last photographs taken of the ship when she was flying the US flag.

Forewarned by these tip-offs, the chief constable managed to head off a number of planned confrontations between the intractable rivals. He also took the bold step in 1935 of banning the Sunday marches, and when a group of 250 Billy Boys set out to defy the rule, Sillitoe orchestrated a plan to outwit them. He loaded up two furniture vans with constables and moved a large contingent of mounted policemen into a side street. The amazement when this force of 'busies' confronted Fullerton and his gang totally deflected them from their purpose and led to headlines in the Glasgow papers the following morning about the triumph of 'Sillitoe's Cossacks'.

The evidence suggests that this particular moment was a turning point in Percy Sillitoe's battle against the Glasgow gangsters, as W. C. Cockroft has written in his biography, *Sir Percy Sillitoe* (1975):

> From this time on the police gained the upper hand. With Sillitoe's backing they clamped down on any breach of the peace with force and offenders received the stiffer sentences for which Sillitoe had asked of the magistrates. A few weeks after the police ambush, Fullerton was charged with assaulting a police officer and given a one-year prison sentence. Leaderless (for no one arose to take Fullerton's place) the Billy Boys fell apart as a gang organisation and, without them, the Norman Conks lost the *raison d'être* for their existence and they, too, disintegrated.

This is, though, too simplistic a conclusion, because groups of Billy Boys and Norman Conks continued to operate in Bridgeton, as the Sheriff Court records indicate. Indeed, their reputation as the hardmen of the area continued for some years, as C. A. Oakley described in *The Second City* (1946):

Sensational reports about gangsters in Glasgow were so common in the 1937–38 period that a private enquiry was begun – the outbreak of the Second World War prevented its completion – into the source from which these stories were flowing. Although no report was prepared, some who took part in the investigation had begun to wonder whether the explanation was not to be found with the large number of Scottish journalists in Fleet Street where a sub-editor coming across a piece about Bridgeton which he knows well passes it for publication.

Whether or not it was Scottish hacks in London furthering the legend, Sergeant Robinson and his 'flying squad' were certainly kept busy and in 1938 were responsible for the arrest and imprisonment of Wilson, McCormack, Fullerton, McCourt and Mulholland after the bloody affray on Glasgow Green.

It is doubtful whether Percy Sillitoe took any more than a passing interest in this case. The arrest and imprisonment of the five men was certainly another satisfactory statistic in his campaign against crime. For Sergeant Robinson, too, it was continuing proof of the efficiency of the 'flying squad' – even if this particular skirmish had given him a few more scars to add to his collection.

The case of the five warring hoodlums would probably have been completely forgotten altogether, but for the fact that these same men were to be reunited in another quite different conflict at the end of their terms of imprisonment in Barlinnie Jail.

Percy Sillitoe had for years been advocating that it was environment, lack of education and employment that produced criminals such as the gangsters. If given the right kind of opportunity, he believed – and said he had proved in the case of George Mooney – even the most hardened villain might make a useful member of society. So when in August 1941, the

War Office, desperate for crew members for the merchant navy, issued instructions to the Glasgow police to look for men, it was entirely in keeping with his nature that the chief constable should have sanctioned Sergeant Robinson and the 'flying squad' to 'recruit' prisoners just released from prison. As he had done so often before, Sillitoe left the method entirely to his vastly experienced men.

But if these particular five men were left with little option but to sign on for service with the merchant navy, who could possibly step into 'the Captain's' shoes to take command of them – and others like them – and turn the lot into a quite different 'gang' to work on the hostile waters of the Atlantic Ocean? Only, in fact, a man in the same mould as Percy Sillitoe, dedicated to his calling, hardened by life and determined to defy the very worst the enemy could throw at him.

Chapter 4

The Brassbounder Rearms

The man who would captain one of the most unlikely crews ever to sail to war was born in the year 1874 within a stone's throw of merchant ships plying their trade to and from the busy port and shipbuilding yards of Glasgow. David William Bone, later to be nicknamed 'the Brassbounder' by his men after they had read of his exploits as an apprentice earning his ticket on the old windjammer sailing ships, entered this life on Dumbarton Road on Clydebank. Soon, the noise of ships' sirens and the sight of vessels from all over the world going up and down the river filled his childhood imagination.

David was the third of four boys, the sons of a local journalist, David Drummond Bone, who worked for the *North British Daily Mail* in Glasgow and specialised in writing on maritime affairs and shipping news. Bone senior was a familiar figure in the Clyde shipyards and possessed a wide circle of friends and contacts among the engineers and architects in the industry. He attended virtually every ship launch and was a guest on many sea trials, his views on new vessels eagerly read by builders and the public alike.

As a father, Drummond Bone was a tower of strength, raising his family alone after the sudden death of his wife in 1887. He was also a significant influence on his third son's fascination with the sea, instilling in the boy's mind a conviction that 'all the best things are just beyond the horizon'.

From the diaries kept by David William Bone, as well as a series of articles that he wrote for the *Glasgow Evening News* in 1910, it is possible to piece together the facts about his early years before fate put him in command of an extraordinary ship crewed by merchant seamen and newly released prisoners from a Glasgow jail.

For a man destined to spend much of his career on some of the most dangerous seas in the world, it was perhaps appropriate that David Bone's first childhood memory was of a violent storm that swept across Scotland when he was just five years old. The family house stood on an exposed stretch of the bank of the River Clyde and for a whole day just after Christmas 1879 the two-storey building was battered by high winds, rain, sleet and snow with such fury that David and his younger brother, Muirhead, were kept indoors.

That night, both boys lay sleepless as the tempest swept across the Kelvin Valley and much of the rest of Scotland. In the early hours, when the storm was at its height, a piece of the chimney suddenly crashed through the roof, narrowly missing the family, and doing such damage that they all had to evacuate the premises and move in with a kindly neighbour until repairs could be made to the shattered building.

Bone never forgot how close to death he came that night – nor the date because, as the newspapers later reported, others were not so lucky. The storm occurred on Saturday, 28 December 1879, and caused the collapse of the Tay Bridge which plunged a train of six coaches with 75 passengers and crew into the turbulent waters below.

Shortly after this drama with the elements, which might have deterred a less resolute youngster from any ideas of going to sea, the Bone family moved to a tenement building at Laurelbank in Partick. The flat on Glenavon Terrace was closer to Glasgow and Bone senior's work at the *Mail*, and afforded fine views of the Clyde as it meandered to the shipyards at

Govan and Linthouse. From here, David Bone was able to watch the vessels with their multicoloured flags moving up and down the river or, alternatively, focus his attention on the great building yards and observe the creation of a ship from iron skeleton to the finished article ready for launching.

David's interest in the sea was encouraged at Hamilton Crescent Public School by the English master, John Main, who, sensing his pupil's inclination, pointed him towards the maritime novels of Frederick Marryat, James Fenimore Cooper, Morley Roberts and W. Clark Russell. The books by Clark Russell, with their stories of voyages in square-riggers and the single-handed achievements of young seamen, fired his mind. Some of their exploits he tried to re-create when on holiday in Loch Goil, making sails for the family punt and striking out across the water.

The lure of the sea grew ever stronger for David Bone, and by his own admission he often played truant from school to walk along the Clyde and 'indulge my romantic fantasy that someday I would go seafaring in a sailing-ship'. In particular, he liked to sit on the bollards at the Queen's Dock and watch the loading of the clipper ships belonging to the Loch Line of Australia.

By now, Bone had realised that by wearing one of the nautical caps given to his father, he was less likely to be spotted by a truancy officer. On one notable occasion he was able to use this disguise to get on board a ship, the *Loch Vennachar*, while it was being loaded and see at first hand what life afloat might be like. During this brief experience – which ended when he was spotted by the ship's mate and summarily ordered off – he also rubbed shoulders with the vessel's young apprentices, known as 'brassbounders' because of their brass-bound clothes and badge cap which distinguished them from the ordinary seamen. He left the ship even more determined to go to sea.

David Drummond Bone could hardly have been unaware of his younger son's determination to be a seaman, and in 1890, when the boy was 'rising 16', he helped him to get an apprenticeship with the City Line of Glasgow, owners of both sailing ships and steamships. Although steamships were then being built on the Clyde in ever-increasing numbers, boys who wanted to be indentured could serve only on sailing ships. Consequently, Bone's first posting as a 'brassbounder' was to the *City of Florence*, a cramped, full-rigged ship, registered at 1,199 tonnes and measuring just 227 feet in length by 35 wide.

The *Florence* was, in fact, notorious among seamen for its lack of storage space to carry even the crew's meagre rations and supplies of fresh water. Later, in one of his articles for the *Glasgow News*, Bone was to refer to his first voyage on the ship as 'Seventeen months of hard sea life, between the masts of a starvation Scotch barque, in the roughest of seafaring, on the long voyage, the stormy track leading westward round the Horn.'

The journey was, though, to prove an experience that would help prepare him for many of the challenges the sea presented later in his career, from battling the worst elements nature could throw up to dealing with the toughest of seamen, men hardened by life and their experiences, not all of them on the sea.

In early November 1890, Bone was sent to Antwerp to join the *City of Florence*, but so cold was the weather that the water around the Afrika Dock froze and it was not until February that the square-rigger with its cargo of cement and coke was able to break free of the ice into the Scheldt and set sail via Cape Horn for San Francisco. During the hiatus, though, he got to know the two other brassbounders and the captain, William Leask, a hardy old Scot from Stromness in the Orkneys who, in the old maritime tradition regardless of whether the man in command is twenty-one or fifty, was known as the 'Old Man'.

Another long-standing tradition among seamen also confronted him on the morning when the *Florence* was due to sail and the crew arrived 'drunk to a man'. Bone recalled this moment in the *Glasgow News*:

> Riot and disorder is the way of things; the Mates, out of temper with the muddlers at the ropes, are swearing, pushing, coaxing – to some attempt at getting the ship unmoored. Double work for the sober ones, and for thanks – a muttered curse. Small wonder that men go drunk to the sea: the wonder is that any go sober!

Once at sea, heading for the warmer waters and the 'barefoot days' of the equatorial seas, Bone worked on his seaman's skills and developed a laconic style of speech, which would enable him to be heard over the noise of the sea. It was to become a trademark remembered by all those who ever sailed with him.

The other seamen on the *Florence* grew to respect Bone with his stocky, rather stiff bearing. He also had a way of standing with his toes turned in a little indicating an inherent stubbornness, while his heavy-lidded eyes gave the impression of a wary man, one prone to careful consideration of his circumstances and possessing an ability never to be caught off guard. In any disputes that arose, David Bone proved himself well able to take care of himself with his fists.

In Bone's diary of this voyage, one entry is marked as a red-letter day. The helmsman of the *Florence* was unexpectedly 'kicked' by the wheel and knocked over. With no one else on the watch, the young brassbounder was given his first 'trick at the wheel'. As the ship was then just south of Diego Ramirez in heavy seas and a roaring westerly gale, it was no mean achievement – although Bone himself remained resolutely modest about the incident, as he did about so many other crucial events in his career at sea.

By the time the *Florence* passed under the Golden Gates of San Francisco and anchored off Alcatraz Island, Bone and the crew had been at sea for 183 days. The dreaming boy who had sat on the Queen's Dock in Glasgow had now been replaced by a hardened, passable seaman sure that he had made the right career choice. His eyes had been opened to the ways of ordinary seamen, too, from the dedicated veterans to the 'hoodlums' – 'them wot signed for a man's wage, and couldn't do a man's work', as one of his crewmates had explained.

In the American port, David Bone had his first experience of a system used to provide seamen for vessels that were short of crew when they were due to set sail. As soon as the *Florence* had laid anchor, several small boats swung alongside and a number of men tried to climb aboard. Despite the best efforts of the mate, several of them succeeded in getting on to the ship and were soon offering the crew free drinks and the chance of better-paid berths on other ships.

These intruders were known as 'crimpers' and Bone stood by fascinated as they went about their obviously well-practised routine. He could never have imagined on that sunny Californian morning that in years to come much the same tactics would be used to crew a vessel he was to sail to war.

Bone discovered later that the 'crimpers' were all under the control of a shadowy figure known as 'Shanghai' Brown who would guarantee to fill the crew of any ship – at a price, of course – by fair means or foul, often the latter. His men were experts at getting seamen fresh from long voyages at sea hopelessly drunk in the waterfront bars of San Francisco and then depositing them, more than likely unconscious, into the hands of those captains prepared to turn a blind eye to the illegality of their 'recruitment'.

It was rumoured that each man taken by this method, known as 'Shanghai Passage', was worth $50. There was little incentive to report the 'trade' to the authorities, though, as 'Shanghai' Brown was said to have all the waterfront magistrates in his pay. David Bone learned that some ship captains had resorted to the use of belaying-pins and even revolvers to prevent the 'crimpers' getting at their men; he was not surprised to learn that the crimpers' activities had resulted in this particular area of America becoming known as the 'Barbary Coast' after the legendary pirate stronghold.

The *City of Florence* remained in San Francisco for several weeks, moored at Mission Wharf, the crew paid off and departed, with the exception of Bone and the other brassbounders. In between carrying out repairs to the ship, the young men explored the city: they visited the waterfront saloons, were tempted by prostitutes in the upper windows of brothels, and wandered through the streets of Chinatown.

When they found an opium den it struck Bone as being nowhere near as sensational as he had been led to believe. There was no sign of the wasted and debauched beings of whom he had been warned: only silent men pulling on their pipes and grinning at the open-mouthed young seamen.

When Captain Leask was finally assigned a cargo of wheat and bags of flour for the return journey to Glasgow, he found himself several men short of a full crew. Bone recalled later that on this occasion even the 'crimpers' could not help, so the resourceful old Scot had to devise his own means of raising extra hands.

The captain opted to try to outsmart 'Shangai' Brown's men at their own game and set off with the second mate for the harbour's drinking dens. In the early hours of the next morning, the pair returned with three unconscious 'recruits' – a Liverpudlian who had grown tired of working in an ironworks, an Irishman to fill the role of cook (or 'food spoiler' as they were generally known), and a runaway apprentice who had decided that life at sea was actually preferable to that on land.

When the trio awoke next morning with thumping hangovers, they were greeted by the grinning face of the 'Old Man' urging them to get to work as the Golden Gate bridge slipped away behind the flapping sails of the *City of Florence* and a final, raucous wail from the siren on Benita Point drifted across the bay...

In the next four years, David Bone broadened his experience as a merchant seaman with voyages from Glasgow on both sail ships and steamships before he received his Second Mate's Certificate. When he heard that there was a vacancy on the Loch Line clipper, *Loch Ness*, he decided to take the position, not without some trepidation because the captain, William 'Bully' Martin, was renowned as one of the most hard-case seamen afloat.

Martin's epithet had been earned from years of dishing out the harshest treatment to all those who served under him and raw brassbounders were food and drink to him. A big, broad-shouldered man with red hair and a neatly clipped beard, he was almost seventy years old at the time, but still ferocious in manner and ready to explode with rage at anyone who did not immediately do his bidding. He had already set many records on the Loch Line clippers plying the routes to and from Australia, and saw no reason why he could not achieve more.

Although Bone was greeted warmly enough by Martin before the *Loch Ness* set sail, he soon felt the lash of the 'Old Man's' tongue when they were at sea bound for Melbourne. As second mate, he was responsible for loading the ship with 320 tons of pig-iron bars, which, unless carefully stowed, would unbalance the vessel. Matters were not made any better by the fact that he had to carry out the operation with a new all-Scottish crew who arrived at the Queen's Dock in the customary state of inebriation. Once out to sea, any slight failure of the *Loch Ness* to respond to the wheel would, he knew, be attributed in the vilest language to the second mate.

Bone had no option but to drive the crew hard and his only relaxation while at sea came in conversations with the small group of emigrant passengers who were on their way to new lives down under. After the glassy calm of the waters around the equator, the ship had to wrestle its way around the storm-tossed Cape Horn, and Bone was the first to admit later that his seamanship gained immeasurably from watching the irascible but hugely knowledgeable 'Bully' Martin in command.

The crew of the clipper were again paid off while the *Loch Ness* remained in Victoria Dock awaiting a return cargo. When this materialised in the form of new-season wool, there was no sign of any of the seamen; they had all drifted away from the port in search of casual labour.

Informed of the predicament, the captain railed at his second mate and determined to find the men himself – even if he had to get them from the local seamen's graveyard! The 'Old Man' was gone all day and just before sunset was seen approaching the ship in a Customs launch containing a pilot and several other men. On deck, Bone and the others could only look on in wonderment. Did Melbourne have its own style of 'Shanghai Passage'? The truth was to prove another portent for David Bone.

Martin had, in fact, gone to the local jail and offered to relieve the governor of the expense of five merchant seamen incarcerated for various acts of unruliness, with the assurance that they would be on the next day's tide bound for far-off Scotland. The prison officer was clearly impressed by this ingenious suggestion and the *Loch Ness* acquired its full complement of crew.

On his return to Glasgow, David Bone, now 24, was ready to qualify for his First Mate's Certificate. He had decided that the time was right to change from windjammers to steam. It might be a world without the crack of sail and the snarl of men like 'Bully' Martin, but he wanted to be nearer home and to marry his girlfriend, Ella Cameron, a Glasgow girl he had known for years. Later the couple would have a son and daughter.

David Bone's decision took him first to the SS *Strathmore*, which chartered between Europe and America and gave him his first taste of the ports of New York and Philadelphia, and then to the SS *Australia*, a steamship of 3,600 gross tonnage belonging to the Anchor Line and engaged in cargo-carrying to India and South Africa. With the outbreak of the Boer War, the vessel was fitted out as a horse transport and Bone never forgot the resilience and patience of the animals as the *Australia* wallowed through stormy seas.

In 1902, after obtaining his Master's Ticket, David Bone cemented his relationship with the Anchor Line by signing up for service on the SS *Massilia*, a new ship of over 5,000 tons specially built to cope with the types of merchandise that could no longer be carried by the old barque-rigged steamers. The vessel, captained by John Thompson, a genial man quite the opposite of 'Bully' Martin, could also carry up to sixty passengers and sailed mainly between Glasgow and Bombay or Calcutta. In all, Bone served ten years with her as second and then first officer.

August 1914 saw the outbreak of the First World War and Bone's appointment to the position of chief officer of the *Cameronia*, a Clyde-built passenger ship of 11,000 tons that could carry a crew of 328 and up to 1,500 passengers. She was widely considered the flagship of the Anchor Line and at that time was being readied to sail for New York with a large number of American citizens anxious to return home, away from the horrors being unleashed in Europe. It was to prove an eventful voyage that would introduce David Bone to the uncertainties and dangers of war at sea.

The anxieties of the passengers and the fact that merchant ships crossing the Atlantic were then on their own and at the risk of attack by German U-boats, put a constant strain on Bone and the other officers. The captain, Francis Wadsworth, was, though, a wily old seaman and his decision to steer a course far

77

from the normal routes, on the edge of the Arctic Circle under the cover of low visibility, made for a safe crossing.

A year later, in August 1915, Captain Wadsworth stood down from the captaincy of the *Cameronia* and David Bone became the commander of his own ship for the first time. In the months that followed he was in command of several Atlantic crossings as the vessel carried cargo, passengers and occasionally Canadian troops taken on board at Halifax or Quebec and bound for Britain. The *Cameronia* also took mail and, occasionally, millions of pounds worth of gold and cash transactions in various forms.

On the early crossings, Bone had nothing more to protect the ship and its passengers from German attack than a few armed riflemen who could be positioned in the lifeboats to watch out for any unusual movements at sea. Later, a six-inch naval gun that had originally been built in 1901 for H.M.S. *Terrible* was mounted at the stern – though her captain had very real misgivings about its effectiveness in action.

The *Cameronia* kept up a busy schedule going backwards and forwards across the Atlantic. On the captain's orders she constantly zigzagged in clear weather and continued to avoid the marauding U-boats as the winter of 1916 saw a terrifying increase in the number of merchant ships lost. Early in 1917, the ship was refitted again to serve as a troopship to take soldiers to Salonika and the luck that Captain David Bone had enjoyed in the Atlantic ran out.

Bone had great faith in the zigzag method for avoiding attack by the German submarines and was doing just this on the afternoon of Sunday, 15 April as the *Cameronia* steamed across the Persian Gulf bound for Port Said. The ship had embarked from Marseilles with 2,700 troops and on this trip was actually being escorted by two destroyers, H.M.S. *Nemesis* and H.M.S. *Rifleman*. On the decks of the steamship men were relaxing in the sunshine, some playing games, others just sunbathing, when a cry of alarm rang out from a look-out on the port beam. As Bone wrote in his subsequent report of the incident, there was nothing at first to see:

> The steersman had no time to act, for a rending explosion almost underfoot threw us all into confusion. The upthrow came on the moment of the torpedo's impact. Broken hatch-covers, coal, shattered debris, a huge column of sea water, soared skyward in a hurtling mass to fall in torrents on the bridge and bear us down. Then, silence for a stunned half minute – only the thrust of the still turning engines marking the heart beats of the stricken ship. Then they too died.

An obituary – not of the ship or any of the men who were lost, but of David Bone himself – recorded most vividly what happened next. The report in *The Times* of Monday, 18 May 1959 stated:

> The troops swarmed up in a near panic, most of them at sea for the first time, making for the boats. Then a small boy [identified as William McKinnon, a bridge-deck messenger] picked up his master's megaphone and in a shrill treble cried, 'Steady you men down there! Steady up. Ye'll no do any good for yersel's crowdin' up the ladders.' They steadied and over 2,500 of them got away. The commander grabbed a stay of the destroyer *Rifleman* which came alongside as his ship went down from under him, and thus he left the bridge that had given him higher standing in his profession.

After the survivors of the torpedo attack had all been landed at Malta by the two destroyers, a headcount revealed that 145 men had been lost, including two of the *Cameronia*'s officers and fourteen seamen. For some nights, Bone was haunted by the faces of the terrified soldiers on the deck after the U-boat had attacked, and in his report he urged the authorities to step up their investigations into finding ways of preventing the enemy submarines getting so close to their victims undetected.

Bone returned to London and after giving a further report at the Admiralty, spent a period of time back on his old stamping ground, the Atlantic, relieving exhausted captains of the Anchor Line. He was pleased to see the ships were at last camouflaged and the crossings were being made in convoys protected by the Royal Navy and, occasionally, by ships of the US Navy.

The Anchor Line, Bone's employer, suffered badly during the war and had lost most of its transatlantic ships by the time peace was declared in 1918. Indeed, it was to be almost two years before the captain was given a new ship of his own – the *Columbia*, which had seen service during the war and been converted into a passenger-carrying ship for 1,400 people.

Many of the travellers on the early voyages to New York were refugees from Europe, and Bone always remembered his first landfall off Sandy Hook, New York, when a sudden rush of excited passengers to the port side of the vessel caused the boat suddenly to list dangerously. Some of the men, women and children were even in danger of being tipped overboard by the tilting, which had been caused in part by the inefficient storing of ballast. Bone could almost hear the voice of 'Bully' Martin roaring in his ears as his crew set about righting the vessel.

The incident did nothing, though, to spoil David Bone's time in New York, a city he had come to appreciate after the perils of the Atlantic. On this occasion, he took several days to explore the Big Apple, in between keeping an eye on the vessel berthed on the North River.

In 1922, Bone was transferred again to take command of the *Tuscania*, a luxury liner catering to the burgeoning trade in ocean cruises. The 17,000-ton vessel was the second-largest transatlantic ship of the Anchor Line and the passenger accommodation had been lavishly furnished. The ship sailed on her maiden voyage in September and Captain Bone, the man who had once rough-housed with some of the toughest seamen afloat, now found himself mingling with the nobility and the wealthy as well as with famous literary figures including Christopher Morley, Walter de la Mare and Joseph Conrad.

After three years spent sailing between America and the Mediterranean ports, the one-time brassbounder moved on to captain the *Transylvania*, a 17,000-ton vessel newly built in Glasgow and designated for cruising. Although the ship's maiden voyage to New York took place in gale-force winds and heavy seas, Captain Bone brought her safely into port and thereupon began travels that would take him to destinations as far apart as Venice and the West Indies until 1939 when the storm clouds of war once again began to gather over Europe.

Captain David Bone was actually crossing the Atlantic from New York to Glasgow at the helm of the *Transylvania* when war was declared on 3 September, 1939. Immediately the news was relayed to him, the events of that terrible day twenty years earlier, when the *Cameronia* had been torpedoed beneath his feet, flashed back into his mind. He wasted no time in ordering the ship to begin zigzagging through the daylight hours and set a course to the far north seeking the fog that would hide the vessel from the eyes of any U-boat commander who might be lying in wait before he reached the safe haven of his home port.

On his arrival in Glasgow, Bone was ordered to hand over the *Transylvania* to the Admiralty as it had been requisitioned to serve as an armed merchant cruiser. If he felt any sense of foreboding for the ship, Bone did not reveal it to anyone. But, in fact, the days of the ship were already numbered. Just a year later, in August 1940, the *Transylvania* suffered the same fate as the *Cameronia* when it was sunk by a torpedo off Bara Head.

As he was now almost 65 – the age at which Anchor Line captains normally retired – David Bone imagined his days at sea were over. But destiny and the demands of the war against Hitler had other plans for him. When he was asked to take a new ship also named the *Cameronia* on a trip to New York, he shrugged off any thoughts of ill-omen and set off across the Atlantic.

The vessel was carrying 400 Scottish and English school-children being sent to America to escape from the war – a complement of passengers not without its own particular problems. Once again, Bone had to make the crossing alone and without an escort – and, once again, thanks he said to 'luck and God' but rather more to his seamanship and knowledge of the dark, grey waters between the two continents, he landed his precious cargo without mishap.

One further voyage remained for Captain Bone before his path would cross that of the ship that would involve him in one of the most curious maritime epics of the Second World War.

This assignment took Bone back to the warm Mediterranean seas with which he had become familiar. Following the German occupation of Greece in 1940, all Greek shipping that was abroad had been requisitioned by the Allies – and among this booty of war was a certain vessel, the *Nea Helles*, which was placed under the management of the Anchor Line. Bone needed only a moment to recognise her as the luxurious *Tuscania*, which he had commanded almost twenty years earlier.

Captain Bone's pleasure at being reunited with the vessel was somewhat dampened, however, when he inspected the engine room and found that a lack of careful servicing by the Greeks had resulted in deterioration to the oil-fuel tanks and the boiler tubes. The effect was that as soon as the journey got under way, dense plumes of black smoke poured out of the ship's funnels – an obvious disadvantage in wartime for any vessel trying to avoid being spotted on the open seas.

There was, though, no time for anything other than emergency repairs to be carried out in the engine room before the re-named *Tuscania* set sail in January 1941 carrying a full complement of troops destined for the Middle East by way of the Cape of Good Hope. Taking up a position at the rear of the convoy, the ship helplessly trailed dense volumes of smoke behind her while Bone never allowed his eyes – or those of his look-outs – to stray far from the surrounding waters.

Fortunately, the vessel made it to the Suez Canal without incident, but there it was decided by the commodore of the convoy that the old liner should go no further. The troops were disembarked on to other vessels and Captain Bone was left to work on his ship until the problem had been overcome. Once the work was completed, the *Tuscania* was turned around and sailed back to Glasgow, making one vital stopover at Gibraltar in June to evacuate a thousand of the island's civilian population.

If, however, Bone imagined when he reached the Clyde again that his problems with a difficult vessel were now over, he could not have been more wrong. In fact, had he known, he might well have accepted more smoke, delays and discomfort in preference to the trouble that lay ahead on his next assignment with a ship named the *George Washington*.

Even more so, had he been aware of the activities of some members of his crew, who were even now getting ready to embark for the same rendezvous...

Chapter 5

A Life of Riley on the Atlantic Ocean

A shipping official with a sense of humour might well have been accused of having chosen Greenock, just along the Firth of Clyde from Glasgow, as the port of embarkation for a section of the future crew of the *George Washington* in the autumn of 1941.

It was, in fact, at this picturesque town with its views across the Gareloch that the infamous pirate Captain William Kidd had been born in 1645. The son of a persecuted church minister, he had gone to sea as a privateer, but despite receiving the then princely sum of $250 from a grateful New York City for acting *against* pirates, he had turned to robbery himself and become the scourge of all shipping around the West Indies until his arrest and execution in 1701.

John Wilson had enjoyed stories about the courageous and bloodthirsty Kidd when he was a youngster, but now had other thoughts in his mind as he and William McCormack and Bill Fullerton stumbled from the train that had brought them from Glasgow, and headed for the docks. Still hungover from the night before, the three ex-cons would have been as little interested in stories about the pirate as they were in the statue of Greenock's other famous son, James Watt, the eighteenth-century pioneer of the steam engine, which they passed as they crossed Clyde Square. What they all fancied was something to drink.

The men had been given travel dockets to report to a ship named the *Pasteur* for their passage to America. None of them knew anything about the vessel and they cared even less – until they saw the name on the bow of a sleek-looking, single-funnelled ship moored out in the Clyde. A low whistle escaped from Wilson's lips. The *Pasteur* was a luxury berth, for sure. They could all be in for a good time, he said, licking his parched lips in anticipation as he spotted a dockside pub.

The Glasgow that the three Billy Boys and two Norman Conks found on their release from Barlinnie had changed considerably in the three years since they had been put inside. The declaration of war had, of course, involved the whole of the United Kingdom, and while Scotland had only had to bear a small share of the brunt of the air war launched by the Germans, most of this share had been directed against Glasgow and the Clyde.

The first daylight raid on the city had occurred on 19 July 1940, followed by a night raid on 18 September when bombs were dropped on George Square, Queen Street Station, and Royal Exchange Square where a building at the east end was completely destroyed. A cruiser, the *Sussex*, berthed at Yorkshill had also been set on fire and caused the evacuation of the nearby Royal Hospital for Sick Children for fear the ship's magazine might explode.

The most serious attacks on Clydeside took place in 1941 when the sound of the German aircraft passing overhead, the anti-aircraft fire and the noise of the explosions was audible even to the inmates of Barlinnie. Statistics reveal that between 13 and 15 March, 1,083 people were killed and more than 1,600 injured, mostly in Clydebank where only seven houses were left untouched by the hail of German bombs As a result, the 50,000 survivors had all to be evacuated.

Greenock itself was the object of raids on 5 and 6 May when 341 civilians were killed and another 312 injured. The fires that broke out seriously threatened the whisky stores and sugar refineries in the locality, but things could have been far worse if any of the hundred or so bombs dropped by German pilots in the vicinity of the Admiralty oil-storage tanks at Bowling – which contained over 12 million gallons – had hit their target.

News of the narrow escape of the whisky stores was naturally greeted with delight by the Bridgeton men in Barlinnie, all just over three months away from release. The public in general, however, stuck resolutely to their war work and the city deserved its growing reputation as 'the arsenal of the Empire'. From the Clyde yards poured merchant ships as well as battleships and aircraft carriers and a huge quantity of smaller vessels including submarines, corvettes, escort ships and landing craft, not forgetting all the work being carried out on countless repair jobs.

The Clyde had also become the chief wartime port of the United Kingdom, handling about 80 per cent of the incoming merchant shipping. Some of the ships were berthed in the Gareloch while others were unloaded at anchor in the lochs along the estuary with little ships and barges ferrying their cargoes of raw materials, munitions and men to and from the mainland. Fleets of fighting ships also assembled on the Clyde and many of these were armed from the enormous quantities of ammunition and equipment being manufactured in and around Glasgow.

All of this activity soon became evident to the men released from Barlinnie on 15 August. Joining the war effort had been something that only Paddy Mulholland had contemplated, but all five had taken the hint from Sergeant Robinson and his men and decided to follow the instructions on the sheets of paper they had been handed by the policemen.

Both the Billy Boys and Norman Conks allowed themselves as long as they dared for drinking sprees before – separately – they took tram rides to St Vincent Place in Glasgow to the offices of the shipping agents listed on the form. There all five were signed on for a ship named as the *George Washington*.

The only good news for the men as they scrawled their signatures on 'Conditions of Service' contracts was that the ship was apparently still being refitted as a troop carrier at the League Island dockyards in Philadelphia and they would not be required to travel across the Atlantic until it was ready. In the meantime, they only had to report to St Vincent Place once a week to draw their 'shore pay', which amounted to £6 10s per week, per man.

Money for doing nothing, Bill Fullerton grinned happily, thrusting his first week's pay into his pockets. Money for boozing, reckoned McCormack and Wilson as they, too, scooped up the notes and coins from the agent's desk, and then hurried to take the twopenny tram ride back to Bridgeton. McCourt and Mulholland were equally happy at receiving such largesse and planned to spend it in much the same way. No *red biddy* [a mixture of red wine and meths] like in the bad old days if this went on, McCourt told himself.

None of the five – with the possible exception of Mulholland – was in any hurry to get to sea, and the temptation to return to crime was strong whenever their money ran out before pay-day. But the implied threat of Sergeant Robinson – who was seen several times in Abercomby Street and Norman Street in the interim – was omnipresent in all their minds.

And so for the hoodlums from Bridgeton week followed week in a haze of alcohol and casual sex. Finally, when they made yet another visit to the shipping agents in St Vincent Place towards the end of September, an official had some news for them. The man, who had grown increasingly fed up with the loud and foul-mouthed 'new recruits,' gave them instructions to report to Greenock where a ship, the *Pasteur*, would take them and other crew members to America. And good riddance, too, he no doubt muttered under his breath.

The *Pasteur* was indeed an impressive vessel, as John Wilson had judged on first sight. A turbine steamer, she had been built in 1937 in France at the yards of Penhoet in St Nazaire. Launched in February of the following year, she had a gross tonnage of 29,253, was capable of just over 25 knots, and required a crew of 540. The accommodation for passengers exceeded 750 berths and included 287 first-class cabins, 126 for second class and 338 for third class.

The high-quality fittings and furnishings on the ship had been installed by August 1939 and her maiden voyage was scheduled for the following month, starting on 10 September. However, instead of travelling in style from Bordeaux to Buenos Aires with a full complement of holiday-makers, the ship went nowhere – the voyage was dramatically cancelled owing to the declaration of war that had been made a few hours earlier.

Instead, the *Pasteur* remained in Bordeaux until the following June when, on the second of the month, she finally raised anchor for her first voyage. The event went unheralded, even in some secrecy, as the ship had been chartered by the French government to transport the country's gold reserves from Brest to Halifax in Nova Scotia to prevent them from falling into the hands of the rapidly advancing German Army.

After successfully completing this mission there was clearly no point in the *Pasteur* returning to France and she was handed over to the British authorities. In August 1941 the ship raised the British ensign under the management of Cunard-White Star and thereafter commenced a series of increasingly perilous cross-Atlantic voyages in aid of the war effort.

On that September morning when the boys from Bridgeton stood on the dockside gazing across the dark waters of the Clyde at the ship, she was still several days away from sailing to Halifax. This was a source of some irritation to her new captain, William Johnson, who knew he would have to keep the new merchant seamen on board for some days before they left port. He had heard gossip that some of these men had been recruited from unusual sources, and rumour had it that several were even fresh out of jail.

Johnson was, though, an experienced seaman and not unduly worried about controlling obstreperous crews. After all, he had been sailing in and out of Glasgow for many years on steam ships. He had dealt before with tough stokers and all the other kinds of men who worked on merchant ships and liked to get drunk when time hung on their hands. Even he, though, had not expected anything quite like the Bridgeton hardmen.

The captain had already seen the *Pasteur*'s manifest and knew that the passengers were, in the main, hundreds of young RAF recruits being sent to training camps in Canada. They, too, liked a drink and could become unruly, but were accompanied by a number of implacable sergeants with voices and tempers to scorch paintwork

Another motorship, the *Llangibby Castle*, was moored not far from the *Pasteur* and would take the overspill of troops bound for Halifax. She was also a luxury ship, some eight years older, and had been requisitioned from the Union-Castle Line in London for troop transportation. The vessel had been built locally at the Harland & Wolff Yards in Govan and had already made several journeys around the world.

Powered by a twin-screw diesel engine, the *Llangibby Castle* was somewhat smaller than her neighbour, with a gross tonnage of 11,951 and a top speed of 14.5 knots. Launched in July 1929, the ship could carry only up to 500 passengers and possessed just two classes: 250 cabins for the well-off and 200 for steerage. Her maiden voyage had been a journey from London to South Africa and back home again in January 1927. Thereafter the vessel had proved popular with cruise-loving families during the thirties until the conflict with Hitler caused her to be reassigned to war work.

Both ships were bathed in weak autumn sunlight as their crews started to assemble. On the deck of the *Pasteur*, three men stood watching the newly recruited merchant seamen being brought out to the ship with a certain interest. They were Jim McGarrity, George Crawford and Pat Docherty who would be eyewitnesses to the dramas that would unfold between Greenock and Halifax in the weeks ahead.

Wilson, McCormack and Fullerton found time for several beers and whisky chasers in a dockside pub before being ordered out by officers from the *Pasteur* already primed about the drinking habits of some of the recent arrivals. Although somewhat sullen about being parted from their drinks before they had been able to get drunk in the best naval tradition prior to embarkation, the three men were not yet prepared to take on the merchantmen. *That* would have to wait until they were safely at sea and far away from any chance of being returned into the custody of Sergeant Robinson.

The crew's quarters on the *Pasteur* proved more luxurious than any of the men had imagined. Bunks with clean sheets, wash basins and cupboards for their clothes. From the galley came the smells of cooking – meat, chicken, fresh vegetables and fat apple pies – a far cry from the fare in Barlinnie, which all went to make the men feel they could be in for a life of Riley.

But despite the luxury, being cooped up on the ship soon paled for the three Billy Boys because they were unable to get a drink. Captain Johnson, already taking precautions to head off any trouble, had ordered that the liquor stores were to remain in bond until the *Pasteur* was at sea.

Jim McGarrity, one of those who had watched the trio join the ship, sympathised with their thirst. A Glasgow man himself and a merchant seaman for over thirty years, he liked a dram, too – and he knew a way to get some.

'It means going ashore, of course,' he explained to the group. 'The thing is, you can't get ashore unless you have some anti-social disease like VD or typhus. Well, there's no way you would fool the ship's doctor about that sort of thing, but you *can* kid him you've toothache and he certainly won't want to mess about removing teeth. So he'll send you off to town to get it fixed.'

The boys loved a good con-trick as much as anyone and agreed to fund Jim on his 'relief' mission. A kitty of £20 was raised between the group and the following day Jim reported to the sick bay with a raging toothache. Years later he recalled how the trick on the *Pasteur* had succeeded:

> It worked like a dream. The doctor fell for my sob story and sent me ashore. I came back later with a suitcase full of liquor for the boys. I also had the start of a massive hangover of my own – and two teeth missing. But it was worth every moment of pain!

The SS *Pasteur* sailed from Greenock on Friday, 26 September. Only those particularly superstitious members of the crew might have been slightly anxious about sailing on a Friday as tradition maintains that bad luck goes with any vessel that puts to sea on that day.

Apart from the fact that the ship was now painted in a dull grey and black, there was little to mark the event from an ordinary peacetime sailing. The crew went about their tasks as usual, although there was evidence that a number had lived up to the tradition of never leaving port entirely sober, even in times of war.

91

The rails of the ship were lined with uniformed RAF men, gazing at the receding coast of Scotland, some of them wondering how long it would be before they would see their homeland again. A few wondered *if* they would ever see the country again with the German forces massed just across the English Channel and rumours of invasion still rife, despite the fact that the fighter pilots had sent the Luftwaffe packing in that marvellous summer of the Battle of Britain. The enthusiasts among them just wanted to get their basic training in Canada over and return as fully fledged pilots ready to take to the skies in the battle-winning Spitfires and Hurricanes.

No such thoughts ran through the minds of Wilson, McCormack and Fullerton. They, too, were still a bit hung-over from the supplies that 'toothless' Jim McGarrity had wangled for them. They were now just waiting for the ship's bond to be opened.

The *Pasteur*, with the *Llangibby Castle* just to her stern, sailed south down the Firth of Forth, around Arran and Kintyre, and out into the North Channel. There, off the coast of Northern Ireland, the two ships turned north and pointed their bows out into the grey, uncertain waters of the Atlantic.

The pressures on the Royal Navy destroyers and cruisers – as many as a thousand merchantmen were at sea at that time – patrolling between Britain and North America against the U-boat menace were so heavy then that the two troop carriers had been instructed to make their own way to Canada. The Battle of the Atlantic had been well and truly joined and merchant seamen everywhere were living on their nerves.

As soon as the two ships were clear into the Atlantic, their captains headed north along a 3,000-mile route that had been telegraphed to them by the Admiralty. It was not a route guaranteed to be free of U-boats, but the weather conditions at the time of year did slightly favour the ships. Even so, experienced skippers like Captain Johnson knew that the ice, fog and inconsistencies of the compass would present their own problems on the route he had been given from the coast of Scotland to the north of Canada. Although it was still September, all seamen in these parts were aware that the Arctic winter season begins to close in during the latter part of October, sometimes earlier, with great ice streams racing southwards, creating a terrible hazard for any unwary vessel.

The *Pasteur* and *Llangibby Castle* were, basically, sailing along the old explorer's route to Hudson Bay: through the same seas that Hudson, Franklin, Parry and Ross had sailed all those years before. Their compass readings were set for Cape Farewell on the tip of Greenland, then across the Davis Strait and dropping south to the welcome sight of Newfoundland and the safe haven of Halifax just beyond.

As the two vessels ploughed away from Britain through heavy seas, their crews may have wondered about the whereabouts of the huge German warships then known to be in these waters, but they saw nothing except open sea. Nor, during the next few days, was the surface of the churning Atlantic disturbed by any sign of the infamous submarine 'Wolf Packs'.

There was, though, undercover activity of another kind going on below decks in the *Pasteur*. The bond on the ship had been opened and the bar with its elegant wooden furnishings, long sweep of mirror and rows of polished glasses intended for the use of luxury cruise passengers, was now doing a roaring trade with the new recruits and servicemen.

To all those from war-torn and rationed Britain, the bar prices – calculated in dollars, but payable in sterling – were nothing less than sensational: twenty cents would buy a double brandy or a packet of good cigarettes. Wilson, McCormack and Fullerton were among the first at the bar in the evening – and the last to go when the roller-blinds were finally pulled down.

It was, of course, inevitable that the three Billy Boys would sooner or later come face to face with the Norman Conks, Bobbie McCourt and Paddy Mulholland, who were also travelling to Canada on the *Pasteur*. According to Jim McGarrity this happened after they had been at sea for only one day:

I was sitting in the bar with a couple of my mates when these two men walked in. As soon as they saw Wilson and his two pals you could see the mixture of surprise and anger on their faces. The lads drinking stopped talking when they saw who had come in and you could have cut the tension with a knife.

I think it was Wilson who spoke first. He wanted to know what the fucking hell the two Catholic bastards were doing on the ship. His face sort of creased up as if all the old rivalry was boiling up in his mind. All three of them got off their seats.

You could tell there was going to be a fight unless someone did something. My mates and I knew that if there was a bad bust-up so early in the voyage, then the captain would close down the bar for the rest of the trip. So we all got up and stood between the two groups.

I knew Wilson, McCormack and Fullerton by then so I said, 'You boys are going to be at sea for a long time. You'd better get used to being together or you'll have to deal with all of us. We're not going to lose our drinking time because of some religious argument which is what'll happen if there is a barney.'

For a moment, McGarrity recalled, there were five pairs of eyes glaring hostility at him. Fists were clenched and unclenched. Only the fact that several other members of the crew had got up on their feet and were edging over to him made him stand his ground.

I went on, 'Look, we're all Glasgow boys. Let's forget our differences, eh? We'll buy you all a drink. What do you say?'

It was Wilson who finally broke the silence. He sort of reluctantly agreed that there was no use fighting here as there were more of us than them. Maybe they should cool down and try and get on with each other? And if we were going to buy them all drinks, he wasn't going to say no!

The situation could easily have got out of hand, but despite the history of trouble between the two gangs, they could see the sense of what I was saying. I think that moment they sort of joined forces the way lots of people from different backgrounds and with different points of view did because of the war.

By the end of that evening, McGarrity recalled, the five men were sharing the same tables and matching each other drink for drink as they edged towards a drunken alliance. The old rivalry still simmered in some of their remarks, but the common situation in which they all found themselves was enough reason to put those to one side. For the time being, at least.

As the *Pasteur* continued across the Atlantic, the five men from Bridgeton found themselves in a similar quandary. For men with big thirsts like theirs, the wages they received certainly did not go far enough. There did not seem to be any opportunities for thieving, either – unless you fancied a long swim back to shore. They discussed the problem for several days and even considered putting the frighteners on one or two of the younger RAF servicemen. They soon realised, however, that the airmen were a tightly knit bunch and, like the crew members in the bar, would heavily outnumber them in any confrontation. Nor were any of them good enough at cards to make a killing. They would have to look to what assets they had in order to raise drinking money.

Merchant seaman George Crawford, who had masterminded the 'toothache' scam, remembered how the problem of obtaining extra drinking money was solved:

It wasn't long after we had been at sea that the cost of paying the dentist's bill, buying the booze and the suitcases to smuggle the liquor on board, left the kitty empty. And there was this fine bar with all those lovely drinks under our noses. We didn't mind the idea of being torpedoed, but we weren't going to die of thirst! So we had to earn our drinking money the hard way.

The 'hard way' did not prove too difficult for such an ingenious group. The solution lay with the RAF recruits, as George later explained:

Below decks there were hundreds of these RAF blokes. Some of them were sleeping as many as sixteen to a cabin. Others were sleeping on the mess decks and some were even trying to get along with hammocks. Then someone suggested we should sub-let our cabins, unofficially of course, so they could get a good kip while we were working the night shift or whatever. When the money started rolling in, we were all happy to kip down in the bar.

The success of this scheme kept all the men in drinking money for a further period – though there was apparently never quite enough to satisfy the thirsts of the Bridgeton boys. Then Bobbie McCourt had another idea. One of his brothers had worked in a café and told him how there was always money to be made from any leftover food. George Crawford remembered this clever piece of business, too:

We noticed that the RAF boys were all on service rations. We were already supplying them with berths, so we said why didn't we feed them with extra grub as well? So we organised a supply of chicken, loaves of bread and jugs of tea from our mess. I borrowed a cook's outfit and the boys loaded me up with trays of freshly cut chicken sandwiches and I sold them to the airmen at one shilling [five pence] a time.

With these two schemes providing the group with a healthy income, they could look forward each evening to spending hours in the *Pasteur*'s bar regaling one another with tales of the past, in particular comparing their wild and violent days. As mile after mile of the Atlantic ocean slipped by, the old enmities between the five hoodlums, which had reached such a bloody pitch on Glasgow Green, seemed to recede.

The pillar of smoke was spotted by a look-out in the still air of one early morning and immediately reported to the *Pasteur*'s bridge. Captain Johnson barely had time to train his binoculars on the sight before the word began to flash around the vessel that there was a ship on fire on the horizon.

After another minute or so, there was a flash of what appeared to be gunfire and the smoke in the distance grew blacker. The binoculars revealed that the vessel was a tanker about six miles away. No other ship on fire burned in quite the same way – a fury of smoke and flame with a unique kind of pyrotechnic brilliance.

The men on the decks of the *Pasteur* – some just standing in groups talking, others playing deck games – stopped in their tracks as the funeral pyre of smoke rose higher into the heavens. Even from this distance, it was quite obvious that there was no hope for the stricken tanker. Nor was there anything the *Pasteur* or her captain could do. To approach the area in case there might be any survivors would only endanger the ship and its passengers. The U-boat that had inflicted this terrible fate might still be in the vicinity, too.

Captain Johnson had specific orders that the safe passage of the airmen was his primary concern and he instructed his navigator to steer a course well away from the tanker, which he knew could go on burning for hours. His duty was not to go hunting trouble, but to get his ship safely across to Canada.

Below decks, the drama had been watched through portholes in complete silence by the Bridgeton boys. Even though they were, as usual, still hung-over from the previous night, the death throes of the tanker brought home for the first time just how close they were to death all the time on the Atlantic. Life in jail had certainly been a lot safer...

Two days later, with over half of the journey complete, the worst fears of everyone on board the two ships was realised. Just as dusk was falling, the grey conning tower of a U-boat rose from the surface of the Atlantic, spume crashing around its hull. The boat was about one and a half miles distant and it appeared about midway between the *Pasteur* and the *Llangibby Castle*. The direction in which it was facing seemed to indicate it was intent on attacking the larger of the two prizes.

Captain Johnson, who had been about to leave the bridge, grabbed his binoculars and read the letters *U 402* on the submarine. His first reaction was one of surprise. Not that the marauder had surfaced, but that it had surfaced without first firing a torpedo. He knew from all the reports he had read that the only warning most merchant ships received of the enemy's presence was of one of the deadly missiles slamming into its superstructure.

As if in slow motion, the German submarine swung its bow to face the *Pasteur* and moments later fired a shot that fell about a hundred yards short. Barely had the spray subsided than another was fired and fell close on the vessel's port quarter.

At every available porthole, faces now were pressed to the glass. Thoughts of the blazing tanker were in every mind. Was it to be their turn now? The flash of the discharge and the unmistakable shrill crescendo whine of shells was followed by the whiteness of their splash as they fell into the ocean. One shell fell almost alongside, a little abaft the funnel, level with the engine room. Spray roared from it as it burst on the water. Fragments seemed to strike against the ship's plating, but no one could see or hear anything in the turmoil of water.

Then up above the water rose some pieces of wood, splintered and torn. As things cleared it was possible to see that the port lifeboat had been shattered. It had been swung outboard in the wartime fashion, hanging ready for use from the davits. Now it was just a broken parody of a lifeboat, no longer of any use.

Up on the bridge, Captain Johnson remained calm, his binoculars still focused on the U-boat. He ordered the helmsman to begin zig-zagging and telegraphed the captain of the *Llangibby Castle* to make off at full speed. Johnson had no gun to reply to the German fire and knew that he could not outrun the submarine if it decided to chase him.

Nor could the captain hope for any Royal Navy destroyer to answer an SOS signal in time. He had to play a mind game with the U-boat's gunlayer hoping to out-think the German as he laboriously corrected his angle of fire after each round of shots fell wide of the mark. Captain Johnson was still puzzled, though, that he had not been torpedoed. As the ship's Parsons-geared turbines clawed through the rolling sea, the submarine fired another twenty rounds, close to the ship, but failing to hit it.

All of a sudden, the firing stopped, and, a few minutes later, the U-boat slowly, almost imperceptibly, began to drop astern and start to submerge. Later, Johnson was to recall the moment in the half-light as 'like a ghost shape stealing away'.

Then it dawned on Johnson *why* the German had not fired a torpedo. *U 402* was probably at the end of a mission and had used up its supply. Perhaps it had been on its way back to the German refuelling and rearming zone in the vicinity of the Cape Verde Islands, when the captain had chanced upon the liner and fancied his chances of sinking – or at least crippling – the vessel with firepower alone. Had the U-boat possessed just one torpedo it might have been a very different story indeed, Johnson decided.

Although the *Llangibby Castle* played no part in this encounter, its Burmeister & Wain diesel engine speeding it on towards Canada, fate had a cruel trick in store for this vessel only months later. In January 1942, while again crossing the Atlantic, the ship was struck by a torpedo and lost both its stern and rudder. However, it escaped without further damage and was able to limp its way to the Azores and dock at Horta on Fayal Island. There the captain swore that the number he had seen on the conning tower of his attacker had been *U 402*.

The German submarine's gun attack on the *Pasteur* had been a traumatic experience for the five Glasgow boys, and most of the other passengers, too, and the sales of alcohol rose sharply in the hours that followed – as did the urgency with which 'cook' George Crawford and his team hustled food to the RAF recruits in order to keep themselves in cash.

Captain Johnson and his officers allowed themselves a little satisfaction at having escaped from the U-boat. Johnson, however, was taking no chances and stepped up the watch, although he had no real need to urge the look-outs to be constantly on the alert. Thankfully, all around the sea remained empty, echoing only to the hard-driven engines as the ship pressed on towards Canada.

As Cape Farewell disappeared behind the *Pasteur*, the *Llangibby Castle* came in view once again, and the two ships crossed the Labrador Basin and began to expect Newfoundland on the horizon. The occasional laugh from the bridge of the *Pasteur* showed the tension was starting to ease. It was the first time most of the officers had been under shellfire and the night after the encounter, Johnson went down to the bar for a drink and found a party, being held by the RAF men in full swing.

All over the vessel, men continued to dwell on the drama of the incident, reliving where they had been at the time, how they had felt and what they had expected to happen. Then, with the approach of the coast of Canada, the sound of bravado once again stalked the decks of the *Pasteur* and discussion turned to what lay ahead in the port of Halifax, Nova Scotia.

Seaman Pat Docherty, one of the trio who had stood on the rail of the *Pasteur* as it took on its ill-assorted passengers and crew at Greenock, had made the trip to Halifax many times before and found himself the centre of attention with the inquisitive Bridgeton boys as they chatted together over drinks on the last evening. Years later, he could recall what he told them about their destination:

> The whole of the bloody British Navy could rest at anchor in the harbour at Halifax. If you can imagine Plymouth and Devonport combined, you'll have some idea of how big the place is!

John Wilson and the others, who had never visited England, could *not* imagine such a place, of course. But they were interested to hear from Docherty that Halifax and the rest of Nova Scotia reminded him a lot of Scotland. There were towns and rivers like those to be seen around Glasgow, and mountains that might have been transported straight from the Highlands.

'There are thousands of navy men and merchant seamen going in and out of the city all the time, lots of them from

Scotland,' he said. 'Their ships are being repaired and refuelled and taking on stuff for the war. The people of Halifax are very patriotic and like to make blokes from Britain feel at home.'

Feeling at home meant only one thing to Pat Docherty's audience – pubs and lots of booze. They had all had more than enough of the sea. Perhaps back on dry land there be would an opportunity to make some more money, one way or another, before the *real* reason for their 'recruitment' began in earnest.

Chapter 6

The Ship Called 'Rip Van Winkle'

Captain David Bone was not at all impressed with the ship that he stood looking at in the League Island Navy Yard of Philadelphia in August 1941. When he had been informed in London that his new command was to be the USS *Catlin*, a requisitioned transatlantic liner, he had not been exactly overjoyed. But the vessel lying at anchor before his eyes on that hot summer morning was, if anything, even worse than he had anticipated.

Bone had arrived in the American city only the previous day after sailing from Liverpool as a passenger on a cargo ship, the *Lockatrine*. It had been a long and arduous journey in a huge convoy of more than fifty ships. It was also a strange experience for him to have no job to carry out. It was, in fact, the first time this had happened since he had sailed across the North Sea to join his very first ship in Antwerp back in 1890.

During the crossing, which had followed a route around the high latitudes near Iceland, there had been one drama when a U-boat pack attacked the sprawling convoy. The *Lockatrine* had been too far away from the encounter for Bone to see anything, but he was later informed that the enemy's torpedoes had caused the loss of two ships. The escorting destroyers had managed to pick up the survivors and transfer them to another vessel in the convoy; the group had then completed the rest of the transatlantic crossing without further incident.

After a fitful night's sleep in the Walton Hotel, Captain Bone awoke anxious for a look at his new command. Following an early breakfast, he took a taxi down the wide thoroughfare known as Broad Street, which ran from City Hall right to the banks of the Delaware River where the shipyard was located.

The driver had immediately recognised Bone as a 'limey' and corrected his instructions to go to the 'Navy Yard', explaining that only a visitor would fail to call it by its proper name: League Island.

As he sat in the taxi, the captain reflected on what he had found out about the *Catlin* from consulting a copy of *Lloyd's Register*. Years later, he would record the emotions he felt that day in these words:

> With some dismay I recognised her as the old German liner, the *George Washington*, a veteran of transatlantic sea travel in bygone days. I had thought her long since condemned to the ship-breakers' yard. I noted the date of her construction at Stettin, 1908, which seemed like something stone-cut on the base of a museum piece!

Bone had no doubt that the vessel had been a splendid ship in her day. But that day was long past and he was now being asked to take her back to sea as a troop transporter with an untried crew and across what was currently the most dangerous stretch of ocean in the world. Once again, he opened the file he had been given on the *Catlin* and looked at the specifications of the vessel as well as a handful of fading sepia photographs taken of her in the days of her prime.

The *George Washington* was, in fact, the second ship to bear that name. The first had been an eighteenth-century American warship, commanded by Captain William Bainbridge, which had spent several years in the mid-1790s patrolling the US coast on the look-out for French privateers. Afterwards, she had carried stores and timber from Philadelphia to French and Italian ports before being sold in 1802.

The second *George Washington* had been designed and constructed specifically as a passenger liner by the Vulcan Works in Stettin for the North German Lloyd Line. A coal burner with twin screws, she had a gross weight of 25, 570 tons and was launched in November 1908. The high-sided, twin-funnelled vessel, 720 feet long, required 350 tons of coal for a day's cruising at a maximum speed of 20 knots.

The file contained photographs of her maiden voyage in June 1909 from Bremerhaven to New York. At the time, the *George Washington* was North German Lloyd's biggest ship – and remained so until the First World War. She was also lavishly equipped to cater for a large passenger list: 568 people in first class; 433 in second; 452 in third and 1,226 in steerage. Her state rooms and dining rooms were said to be among the most luxurious afloat. To handle this giant, a crew of 585 men was required.

For the next five years, the ship made regular transatlantic crossings, packed with European and American passengers travelling 'in the lap of luxury'. Then came the outbreak of war in 1914, at which point the vessel's captain sought refuge in New York, then a neutral port.

However, when America herself entered the war in 1917 as a result of U-boat strikes on US shipping in the Atlantic, those members of the German crew still living aboard the *George Washington* attempted to sabotage her. The men managed to do serious damage to the boilers and cylinders before US Navy officials were able to get aboard and intervene.

On 6 April 1917, the *George Washington* was towed to the New York Navy Yard and there converted into a transport ship for the US Army. Under the command of Captain Edwin T. Pollock, she sailed with her first complement of soldiers in

December 1917. During the following two years the former liner made a total of eighteen transatlantic voyages in support of the American Expeditionary Force in Europe.

The ship made international news in December 1918 by carrying President Woodrow Wilson and other American representatives to the Peace Conference in Paris. On this crossing – and in contrast to previous voyages and those that would follow during her time in the British Navy in the Second World War – the *George Washington* was protected by the huge US battleship, the *Pennsylvania*, plus nine other battleships and even several destroyers, all of which escorted her safely into Brest harbour on 13 December. As one observer noted, the fleet around the president's ship that day presented 'a pretty impressive demonstration of American naval strength'.

The ship's log for this period also records that the liner carried the Assistant Secretary of the Navy (and President-to-be) Franklin Roosevelt to France in January 1919; and on 24 February returned President Wilson to the United States. She again made a transatlantic crossing with Wilson on board in March of that same year, returning him home at the conclusion of the historic conference in July at which he had played a major role in helping to establish the League of Nations.

The colourful career of the *George Washington* continued in the autumn of 1919 when she carried the king and queen of Belgium and their party from France to New York, arriving on 2 October. After a series of state functions and special visits in and around the city, the royal couple returned to Brest on her on 12 November.

When the decision was taken to decommission the ship on 28 November 1919, it was estimated that during her operational period of more than a decade she had transported over 48,000 passengers to Europe and brought almost 34,000 back to the United States. As a result of this arduous schedule, orders were given that the vessel should be refitted and overhauled.

This work was carried out in the dry dock of Tietjen & Lang in New York, reducing her gross weight to 23,788 tons. The ship was thereafter charted by the US Mail Steamship Company with whom she made just one transatlantic voyage from New York to Bremen, before the company was taken over by the government in 1921 and re-named the United States Lines.

For the next ten years, the ageing *George Washington* continued to cross and re-cross the familiar ocean between America and Europe until, in November 1931, she was withdrawn from service and laid up at a place called Solomon's Island on the Patuxent River in Maryland. There, indeed, she might have remained, rusting and forgotten, but for the outbreak of another war.

Early in 1941, as a result of research by the naval authorities to discover the number of vessels that might prove useful as troop transports, it was decided by the US government to reacquire the *George Washington*, and reactivate her once again. On 28 January, her engines were fired and her anchor raised from the muddy floor of the Patuxent River. A brief – but in hindsight very revealing – record in the archives of the Office of the Chief of Naval Operations in Washington describes this fateful moment in the ship's history:

The *George Washington* was re-acquired for Navy use from the Maritime Commission on 28 January 1941 and commissioned *Catlin* in honour of Brigadier General Albertus W. Catlin, USMC. It was found, however, that the coal-burning engines did not give the required speed for protection against submarines and she was decommissioned on 13 March 1941.

This, then, was the extraordinary ship that Captain Bone stepped out of his taxi to view on an August morning five months later. He had read in his file of the ship's earlier failure to make the grade and could not repress a moment of doubt as to whether she might not do so again. But he had his orders.

The League Island Navy Yard was an impressive facility by any standards and he could see at once why it was said to epitomise the history of American sea power. Originally, the ships of the infant nation's navy had been berthed at the Philadelphia Yard (then at the foot of Federal Street) and set out from there to defend the country against French privateers. Following the American stand on freedom of the seas in 1812, the yard then built, outfitted or repaired many of the stout wooden vessels that took on the might of the British Navy.

With the passing of these oaken warships, the yard proved unsuitable for the construction of iron vessels and in 1862, the 923-acre League Island was transformed into the new centre for building and servicing such vessels. The building of a large number of ships for the Federal Navy during the Civil War resulted in the United States becoming the dominant sea power for the next decade.

During the First World War, the League Island Yard was greatly expanded, and its facilities modernised; as a result many large steam ships were built there. It quickly became the third-largest yard in the country, with the added advantage of having steel mills and coal mines located nearby. As the Navy's only fresh-water yard on the Atlantic seaboard, it was claimed to be ideal for preserving steel ships against the rapid corrosive effects of salt water while they were being serviced.

As Captain Bone walked through the main gates he could see the yard's three dry docks. The largest, which was able to accommodate ships up to 1,000 feet in length, had a water capacity of 53 million gallons and boasted two of the world's largest electric cranes, each over 230 feet high and capable of lifting 350 tons. There were also a number of piers, and, tied up at Pier 5 was the reason for his long journey from Britain, the *Catlin*, lying, as he later wrote, 'lubberly and forlorn'.

Before inspecting the ship, the captain had a meeting at the office of the admiral commandant, Rear Admiral Watson, the man responsible for handing her over to the British. It did not take Bone long in conversation with the gruff but knowledgeable American sailor to realise that the *Catlin* was not popular with the authorities in the dockyard. Indeed, she had a reputation for being somewhat difficult – almost a jinx – and was known to seamen and shipbuilders alike as the 'Rip Van Winkle.' From the brief glimpse that he had already had, Bone suspected he knew why.

It was, of course, as a result of the Lend-Lease Agreement which President Roosevelt had drawn up with Winston Churchill in early 1941, that Captain Bone was about to take command of the ship for use as a troop carrier. First, though, she had to be refitted, her engines overhauled and tested all over again. Bone hoped he would have an opportunity to advise on the refitting and just prayed the ship would turn out seaworthy *and* a little faster.

As Captain Bone glanced out of Rear Admiral Watson's window at the *George Washington*, he could be forgiven for wondering if this was really what Roosevelt had in mind when he had dreamed up the agreement? Certainly, the repairing of British warships and merchantmen in US dockyards was working well and the funds had already been allocated for the building of 58 additional shipping ways and 200 extra ships. There was no mention, as far as he could recall, of refloating old hulks.

But beggars could not be choosers, Bone told himself. This was to be his ship and he would make the very best of it as he had always done. He was somewhat relieved to hear from Rear Admiral Watson that work to make the decommissioned liner ready for service was underway and a completion date of October had been pencilled in. Captain Bone, though, sensed from Watson's tone that this was an optimistic rather than a realistic estimate. But perhaps it was now time for him to see for himself and discover the best – and the worst – about his new command.

When Captain Bone walked out of the League Island Yard offices he could hardly fail to spot typical examples of the Lend-Lease Agreement in practice. Along the piers there were a number of Royal Navy corvettes and sloops swarming with workmen busy with repairs, not to mention several battleships riding at anchor in the harbour.

The vessels were immediately identifiable by the White Ensigns fluttering on their bows and the very sight of them lifted the captain's spirits. Grandest of all was the battleship H.M.S. *Furious* across the other side of the basin, which was also evidently in the middle of a refitment. Bone knew all about the exploits of this battle-hardened veteran of the Atlantic.

As he headed towards his new command at Pier 5, Bone noticed she was still flying the American Stars and Stripes and the pennant of her present captain, Lieutenant-Commander Zachary Taylor Jones, USN. He would remain in charge of the vessel until the transfer.

When Captain Bone met Lieutenant-Commander Jones he found a veteran of the service with an unflappable nature and dry sense of humour. Jones also proved an invaluable source of information and inspiration, not to mention patience, for the captain during the days and weeks that were to follow.

Lieutenant-Commander Jones was in a position to tell Bone something more about the vessel's history before he had brought her from Solomon's Island to Philadelphia in March. Apparently, during the years she had lain on the Patuxent River alongside a collection of similar old hulks, it had been common gossip that she would most likely be towed away and broken up for scrap. The Japanese had allegedly even made an offer for the vessel which the Maritime Commission had rejected – only, it was said, because the bid was too ridiculously low!

Although the people living on Solomon's Island would have welcomed the disappearance of the old German liner and any of the other wrecks as this would free up the rich oyster beds in the river, it never quite happened. Lieutenant Jones said a naval maintenance party visited the ship from time to time as did maritime inspectors from the US government.

Yet, despite the rust on the *George Washington*'s structure caused by lolling on the river tides for all those years, the steel hull was still in good condition. The decision to keep her in reserve seemed a sound one when, later, war broke out in Europe, and America began to look at her own resources of ships and weaponry.

Jones admitted to Captain Bone that the verdict from the naval operations office about the lack of power from the coal-burning engines had been correct. But these engines were now undergoing a thorough overhaul and it was hoped this would enable the ship to become proficient once more. The lieutenant-commander invited Bone to look over the vessel for himself.

The *Catlin* was not, in fact, quite upright at Pier 5, but lying at an inclination from the dockside. This enabled the captain to see at a glance the lower plating. An area of the incrustation of years had been scaled off and the steel underneath was bright and uncorroded, confirming the opinion that the hull had years of life remaining.

However, some of Bone's other first impressions did not please him. The four masts of the ship, he noticed, had been shortened for no reason that was apparent to him, giving the whole ship a rather unkempt look. Things did not get any better when Bone went aboard, as he later confided in his diary:

It was about noon when I climbed the long gangway to board her and the inactivity of the mid-day break

111

heightened the appearance of disorder on her littered and deserted decks. I thought of all the hard labour involved in restoring her to shipshape condition and pondered the Rear Admiral's enquiry concerning the employment of our British crew.

Rear Admiral Watson seemed particularly interested in the date on which the British crew would join to relieve the four US officers and over sixty naval ratings who had at that moment the care and maintenance of the ship. I could not assure him of a definite date, but reported that my crew was on its way out to join.

The captain, of course, knew from his own experience that it was never a good idea to have a bunch of merchant seaman idle in port. If there was nothing for them to do on the boat, or they had been signed off, then they tended to spend their time drinking and running the risk of getting into trouble. He certainly had enough on his plate at the moment and did not want a crew on the loose in Philadelphia until the ship was ready to go to sea.

No sooner was Captain Bone on board the *Catlin*, however, than he was greeted by two faces he was pleased to see. They were both merchant officers from the Anchor Line who had already arrived to provide what help they could in the reconditioning as well as familiarising themselves with the vessel. The men, Staff Captain John Steuart, a career seaman, and Bone's old friend, Chief Engineer James Spencer, who had served with him before, wasted no time in telling him of their misgivings.

Steuart believed that, based on his own inspection of the ship, the estimated completion date was impossible. Spencer agreed with this and told Bone that the boilers were in a far worse state than had been reported and he was not at all happy with the dockyard's plans for reconditioning them.

Bone was enough of a diplomat to know that there was no point in complaining to the League Island naval authority. They had more than enough problems dealing with ships for the US Navy without a bunch of limeys moaning about vessels that they were damn near being *given* by the American taxpayers! In any event, experience had taught him that the repair of an old ship was in actual fact a more difficult job than constructing a boat from the keel upwards.

So the three men put their heads together to see what help they could offer in order to make the lives of Rear Admiral Watson's men and their own easier. James Spencer had already learned to his dismay that most of the *George Washington*'s original blueprints, plans and diagrams of the systems, engines and boilers had either been destroyed by the German crew's attempted sabotage in New York, or had been lost over the years the vessel had been in service.

The sum of all these difficulties was that many repairs were having to be done in a makeshift manner based on new measurements and utilising materials that often differed from the original. Not surprisingly, it was already evident that some of the hard-pressed American craftsmen were less than enamoured with their task and were not getting ahead as quickly as had been hoped.

However, it was working on the twelve huge, coal-burning boilers – now more than 33 years old – that presented the dockyard workers with the 'father and mother of all headaches', according to Bone. Once again he subsequently committed his thoughts about this time to paper:

Certainly the boilers were well constructed, but all metal grows old, and boilers – subjected to frequent alternations of great heat and cooler temperatures – perish more quickly than less actively excited components of a ship. It was admitted that this heart of the old vessel was diseased, but the ship doctors with their improved panacea of electric welding held to the considered opinion that the boilers could be made serviceable. Venturing to express my doubts, that submission was brushed aside by the experts... who would not have to sail in the ship.

Captain Bone could certainly not have realised then just how accurate his prognosis was to prove. But as he left Spencer and Steuart at work later that afternoon and returned to his hotel, another headache, which might also reach 'father and mother' proportions, was beginning to intrude into his thoughts. It was a predicament that had not confronted many captains for years: where would it be possible to find the stokers able to shift 40,000 shovelfuls of coal a day at sea? The breed of seaman whose strength and stamina at feeding steamship fires had created many records across the Atlantic had, he knew, died out like the old windjammer sailors he had first gone to sea with. Indeed, the introduction of oil fuel had virtually done away with physical labour in the engine room and the traditional 'firesmen' – as Bone had personally known them – were no more.

But Captain Bone had already proved himself on many occasions to be equal to a challenge. He remembered the man who had been his leading stoker on the *Columbia* back in 1920, the redoubtable Archie Roberts. A telegram to the Anchor Line offices in Glasgow established that the veteran merchant seaman was still hale and hearty, and Bone at once invited him to join the crew of the *George Washington*. Roberts replied just as quickly that he would be pleased to join his old captain.

Archie Roberts was the archetypal stoker. Glasgow-born, stocky, with broad shoulders and huge hands, he came from the tough-as-old-boots school of below-deck seamen who would fall out of a waterfront bar on to their ship and then amaze anyone who cared to watch with their skill at the furnace foot-plate. The speed with which he could shovel coal into the voracious fires was legendary, and for years Archie prided himself that there was not a trimmer born whose demands for more coal he could not meet, no matter how long his shift might be.

There were stories told among Scottish merchant seamen that there was no sea too turbulent, or ship that rolled so wildly, as to stop Archie Roberts' rhythmical delivery. His sheer strength and versatility – not to mention his legendary capacity to take a drink – had deservedly earned him the position of leading stoker and he was a man whose authority no one would readily dispute. Archie's reputation of being able to make any man perform the duties for which he had signed on was not based purely on his blistering tongue, either.

The seasoned stoker had an intensely practical approach to his job, which Captain Bone admired. When he was told of the predicament facing the commander, Roberts agreed that recruiting experienced assistant stokers for the ship at this crucial stage of the war and at this distance would be nigh on impossible. But the assurance he gave Bone rang in the captain's ears: 'Just gie me the bodies – hands and feet – and I'll man the bunkers and stokehold for ye.'

In fact, a number of those recruited bodies – hands and feet and all – were already busy on the North American continent. And while they may not have been keeping any furnaces blazing, they were certainly raising the temperature of the Canadian authorities to boiling point.

Chapter 7

Mob Rule in Montreal

The port of Halifax, which emerged slowly out of the October morning mist into the view of the passengers and crew of the *Pasteur*, did, indeed, have similarities to Scotland as Pat Docherty had told the Bridgeton boys. Its beautiful setting and magnificent harbour – the second-largest natural harbour in the world – would no doubt have begun drawing immediate comparisons with the Clyde region back home, except that all five of them were still sleeping off their drinking session of the previous night.

As the ship moved slowly towards its berth between a large number of other merchant ships and naval vessels riding at anchor, it was evident that here was a place steeped in history. A history, in truth, tied enduringly to that of Britain, as the very name of the province, Nova Scotia (New Scotland) indicated.

In fact, it had been the Scottish king, James IV – subsequently James I of England – who had issued a charter in 1713 to Sir William Alexander, the Earl of Sterling, to colonise the stretch of land between New England and Newfoundland, 'to be holden of us from our kingdom of Scotland as a part therof'. The king, it is said, chose the apt name for the new territory, although it was mainly discharged English soldiers and sailors who founded Halifax as its capital in 1749.

116

The huge sweep of bay and flat hinterland proved to be ideal for a port, and by the eighteenth century, Halifax had become the centre of a prosperous fishing industry. That it was navigable all year round – later becoming known as 'The Winter Gateway of Canada' – was also a factor in it being turned into a naval base in 1758 and used as the starting point for expeditions across the border during the American Revolution.

Nova Scotia's scenery and its damp, temperate climate made it so like parts of Scotland that colonists were soon pouring across the Atlantic: no fewer than 50,000 Highlanders were lured to new lives in the early nineteenth century. Cape Breton at the northernmost point of the province was soon being referred to as 'The Road to the Isles' and so large were the numbers of immigrants that in time it was a virtual Scottish colony. Indeed, there were said to be so many Macdonalds living in Nova Scotia that they were known simply by their nicknames!

Halifax, as the Canadian city geographically closest to Britain, had played a vital role as a naval and air base in the First World War, and was now doing so again in the Second, with vast numbers of fighting ships and merchantmen making full use of its facilities to get repairs and take on fresh supplies.

Local history records that several times in 1918, German U-boats came right into the Halifax basin to attack Allied shipping. But on one memorable occasion two of these submarines were hit by the guns of the defenders and the crews taken prisoner. The Germans were subsequently imprisoned in cells in the moated, star-shaped old fortress, the Citadel, which was 'full of rats as big as cats', according to one contemporary account.

The capital's participation in the Great War had not been without its cost, however. In December 1917 a munitions ship collided with a freighter while manoeuvring in the Narrows and the resulting explosion blew the harbour slope off the map, killed 2,000 people and shattered just about every pane of glass in the city. Memories of the event – the greatest human-caused explosion prior to that at Hiroshima – were still vivid when the city was again thrust into the front line of the Atlantic war in 1939.

Indeed, just five months before the *Pasteur* reached harbour, the new conflict had seemed to be getting dangerously close when the awesome German battleship, the *Bismarck*, was thought to be heading for the port. Anxiety grew after the ship had sunk H.M.S. *Hood* near the coast of Greenland, but it was thankfully intercepted by the battleships *King George V* and *Rodney* off Newfoundland and finally sunk in mid-Atlantic on 27 May.

As the summer of 1941 turned to autumn, the tempo of repairing and restocking British merchant and naval ships increased and even as the *Pasteur* steamed into the harbour in the early hours of the morning, workers could be seen scurrying like ants over dozens of the vessels, all camouflaged in grey paint, many bearing the scars of encounters with enemy firepower. Not for nothing was it reputed to be the busiest harbour in the world.

The sky was grey and there was a chill in the air as the *Pasteur* dropped anchor. The RAF recruits were the first to be disembarked from the ship and it was nearly midday before the five men from Bridgeton were roused from their bunks. The boys' initial grumbles and curses stopped when they realised the ship had docked and they would soon be free to go on shore – and start drinking.

John Wilson and Bill Fullerton were the first dressed and roused the others. All five stumbled up on to the deck: it did not occur to any of them to wonder whether the alliance they had formed in drunken revelry on the boat might now be broken or that they might go their separate ways on Canadian soil.

A boat was drawn up alongside the *Pasteur* to take the crew and recently recruited new merchant seamen to shore. Their initial destination was Pier 21 which, ever since 1928, had been the point of entry for more than half a million immigrants, refugees and troop ships. Known as the 'Front Door of Canada', it struck Bobbie McCourt as a place containing despair and expectation in equal proportions.

Passing through customs and being given details as to where to report for instructions and, more importantly, to pick up their wages, seemed to the men to take an eternity. At least they learned that they were going to be in Halifax for a while before moving on to Montreal and from there across the border into the US and a rendezvous with their ship in Philadelphia.

Outside the building, the first sight to meet the eyes of the five Glaswegians was the huge CNR Railway Station. To the left was Water Street, a twisting thoroughfare that ran along the edge of the harbour past dozens of wharfs and docks full of vessels of all shapes and sizes.

The men's first impressions of the city confirmed what Pat Docherty had told them. The place *did* look like Scotland. Especially the docks, which were very similar to those they had left behind in Glasgow. And there you would be sure to find one thing in plentiful supply – pubs.

For almost a quarter of an hour the group trudged along the road without seeing any sign of a bar. They were getting thirstier by the minute when they finally stopped a dock worker evidently on his way home after a night shift. His reply to their enquiry was the first indication that things in Halifax were not *quite* the same as in Glasgow. 'Sorry, fellas, there are no pubs – this city is dry,' he explained. 'If you want a drink you'll have to get it in your hotel.'

The expressions on the faces of the five merchant seamen told their own story. The Canadian looked at the men for a moment and then spoke again: 'But, hey, there is a beer tavern at Purdy's Wharf. It's a way up the street, though.' The docker explained that the tavern was in the old part of the city on

Upper Water Street near the Halifax to Dartmouth ferry. They just needed to keep walking and they couldn't miss it, he added with a smile before going on his way.

'That *bam-pot* Docherty nay said nuthin' aboot having ae this trouble to get a fookin dram,' Fullerton swore.

What the five Scotsmen had just discovered was why the Canadian Liquor Laws had become an unfailing source of music-hall jokes and proved to be the one factor to upset visitors from the UK more than the absence of great buildings, theatres or museums. Nowhere could you find anything remotely resembling the cheerful, uninhibited atmosphere of a pub, a fact that inspired a certain British corporal serving in the Northwest Mounted Police to utter the immortal line, 'In Canada there are no barmaids – the society is not sufficiently educated for them.'

The absence of pubs had been caused years before by a powerful anti-alcohol movement with strong religious under-tones who were known by their opponents as the 'Iced-Water Baptists'. Such was their power that they were able to label all drinking a sin and introduce the Liquor Laws, which declared that if a person wanted to sin, 'they must do so in private'. The result was that alcohol could be purchased only in government-controlled 'Retail Stores', where all bottles had to be wrapped up before leaving the premises and not opened until the purchaser was safely home; alternatively, alcohol was available in rigidly controlled, men-only 'Beer Taverns'.

After a long walk along Water Street into what was clearly the older section of the city, with its cobbled roadways, stone walls and jumble of waterfront warehouses, relics of an earlier colonial age, the five Glaswegians finally came across a building unobtrusively labelled 'Beer Parlour' just off Duke Street. The boys pushed through the door and stopped in amazement at what they found inside.

The tavern was a gloomy bunker of a room without a single window, picture or poster to break up the monotony. Huddled around metal tables, small groups of men sat drinking together with the occasional despondent-looking figure on his own. In front of them all stood clusters of half-pint glasses in varying states of emptiness. Hardly a word was being spoken by anyone.

At the far end of the room, half a dozen waiters were leaning against a long, stainless-steel bar making the occasional comment to the 'beverage dispenser' standing behind. They all looked around as the Bridgeton boys entered. Their sullen stares indicated at once that they had experienced visiting merchant seamen before. Two of the waiters broke away from the rest and walked over to the newcomers.

'You guys just landed?' the bigger of the pair asked and without waiting for an answer indicated two empty tables near the far wall. 'Only four to a table. We just sell half-pints – but you can have two at a time. You got the cash?'

The Scots looked at each other. They had never been spoken to like this in a boozer *ever*. John Wilson, bristling, was about to speak, when the surly waiter spoke again. 'Any trouble and you're out. You won't get served. And we don't allow any moving from table to table or any noise. Got it?'

The five men were lost for words. Could this *snide* be for real? Could they do *onything* for Chrissakes?

Despite his annoyance, Wilson summed up the position first. With a nod of his head, he indicated to the other four that they had better sit down or they wouldn't get served and he for one was damn thirsty. He put his hand into his pocket and showed the waiter a handful of Canadian currency. 'Gee us some bevvies.'

The waiter nodded and turned away to the bar without waiting for an order. Wilson, McCormack and Fullerton took one of the tables and McCourt and Mulholland the one adjoining it. When the waiter came back with ten glasses of the local Keith beer balanced on a large tray, the Bridgeton boys drank quickly and in silence.

Once the waiter had returned to the bar and the boys had slaked their thirst they began to talk hesitantly to one another. It was clear from the attitude of the surly waiter that he was just looking for an opportunity to bounce them out and the others were big and ugly enough to wade in if there was any trouble.

As he drank his half-pint, McCormack's eyes ran down the notice on the wall headlined 'Part III of the Regulations of the Nova Scotia Liquor Control Act', which added several more 'don't-do's' to those the waiter had already muttered.

'Fook me, you cannae even stand oop wi a glass in yer hand,' he whistled through his teeth. 'An look at that: na loitering, na goin from table to table without permission, and na singin'. Why don't they ban fookin' talking, too?'

When the waiter who had served them glanced across, Wilson urged his friend to quieten down. If they got thrown out of here there would be nowhere else to drink.

As the day wore on, however, the boys grew mellower and their capacity to drink and the generosity of the tips they handed to the waiter gradually softened the man's attitude. He even began making jokes about the drinking laws – setting them chuckling with disbelief about the man in Ontario who had been fined for drinking a glass of beer on his front lawn, 'because folk could see him!' The waiter even suggested a cheap hotel on nearby George Street which was very used by merchant seamen and which would allow them to take bottles into the rooms.

Just before six o'clock, the door of the tavern opened again and a man who was clearly the local policeman walked in. As he moved between the tables, the cop toyed suggestively with a pair of handcuffs and then stopped between the two tables occupied by the Scots. After asking if they were here for long and being told they were in transit for Montreal, he grunted that they should stay out of trouble or they would find themselves spending time in the cells. William McCormack was close to rage at hearing the implied threat. Any *busie* who spoke to him like that back in Glasgow would have run the risk of a serious bashing.

The policeman looked at his watch. 'Nearly 6 o'clock,' he boomed across the room. 'Closing hour. Drink up.'

The order was yet another example of the draconian liquor laws in Halifax. All beer taverns had to close between six and seven in the evening – the reason being, someone had once joked, because it made sure that the 'sinful' drinkers went home for at least an hour!.

The five Bridgeton boys emptied their glasses and rose to their feet. The sooner they got some rooms in a hotel and were free to drink when they liked the better. And the sooner they were out of Halifax probably the better, too. Though what if Montreal turned out to be just as bad?

In fact, the quartet from Bridgeton remained in the city for just over two weeks. Twice they had to walk back along Water Street to Pier 21 and the offices of the shipping agent to draw their week's wages. Most of this money was spent in the tavern or on bottles of liquor purchased at a 'Retail Store' on Brunswick Street and dutifully carried back to the hotel in their plain brown paper wrapping. It was probably the quietest and most-law abiding period the five hoodlums had spent in years – outside of jail, that is.

On a bright November morning they caught a train at the CNR Railway Station on South Street. They were headed for Montreal and the next stage of their journey. Once again, the men found problems in slaking their thirsts. The liquor laws which so bedevilled the city had also conspired to make life difficult for barmen on the transcontinental trains and, in turn, their passengers.

By law, the tax on all the drink consumed in a Province while the train was in transit belonged to the regional government. As a result, the bar cars would carry as many as nine separate and identical lockers of alcohol to be sealed or opened as soon as these invisible frontiers were crossed. One amusing effect of this was that when trains passed from, say, the 'wet' province of British Columbia to 'dry' Alberta, halfway through the Rockie Mountains, the bar staff would be forced to call, 'Drink up, please' and slam down the shutters.

On the train, the five Scots were reunited with a number of the other men from the *Pasteur* and settled down for a good session in the bar car as the train steamed across Nova Scotia, New Brunswick and on via Quebec to the island city of Montreal. The scenery was dominated by wooded terrain interspersed with stretches of pasture and ploughland. Occasionally, a village came into view, complete with hip-roofed barns built to allow the heavy snows of winter to slide off easily and keep the livestock inside safe.

Several times, the train made stops at small wayside stations to take on coal and water. Much to their surprise, the Bridgeton boys found themselves being fêted as heroes on the way to war. Local people offered them gifts of food and fruit and, occasionally, rye whisky. It was the first time the hardmen from Glasgow had ever been treated with admiration rather than the looks of apprehension and fear that normally greeted their appearance.

There are stories that some of the recruits from Britain on this cross-Canada journey were so taken by the countryside and the appeal of the places where bright lights winked invitingly beside the track – in stark contrast to the blacked-out world they had left behind – that they were unable to resist the temptation and left the train never to be seen or heard of again.

Some, it has been suggested, crossed the border and began new lives in the vastness of the American Midwest, far away from the threat of war. True or not, there is evidence to support this in the names of merchant seamen who boarded the Halifax to Montreal train and remained unaccounted for long after it had reached its destination. Others did reappear a few days later, rather hung-over and in need of a shave, having enjoyed Canadian hospitality a little too freely.

During the journey, Bill Fullerton won his four companions a round of drinks with the best story about boozing in Canada. He retold a story he had heard from the waiter in Halifax about the trains that ran through a tiny 'dry' hamlet called Bowmanville, in Ontario. It apparently took just two minutes to cross the hamlet, but during that time the time the poor barmen had to close down and then reopen their bars!

All the drinkers on the train were, though, glad to hear from their barman that Quebec Province in which Montreal was located had a much more broad-minded approach to licensing laws, and that there were any number of good taverns to be found in the city. Wilson, McCormack, Fullerton, McCourt and Mulholland left the train at the magnificent steel-and-glass-roofed Windsor Station in much the best spirits since they had docked 680-odd miles away in Halifax.

In Montreal, once again, the Glasgow boys found things to remind them of home in both the city's appearance and history. The ocean-going vessels on the St Lawrence Seaway were an immediate reminder of the Clyde, as was the busy harbour with all the evidence of repairing and loading vessels along the ten miles of berths.

Here, too, the ex-cons were to learn about curious laws dating from the past – though not, thankfully, focusing on a man's penchant for drink. Rather that a man was obliged to maintain his garden by ensuring he had at least three trees and cut his lawn once a week (winter excepted)!

The largest city in Canada, Montreal is situated at the foot of Mont-Royale, 800 feet high, on an island in the St Lawrence River about a thousand miles from the sea. Originally it was an Indian village; in 1642 the French established a settlement called Ville St Marie, but in 1760 this was captured by the British. Following the arrival of the hard-headed Scottish fur-traders of the Northwest Company, Montreal – as it became known in the eighteenth century – began to be transformed into a major commercial centre.

Legend has it that three families – the McGillivrays, the McTavishes and the Frasers – laid the basis of the great city, coupling Scottish graft with French style to form a unique community, and building themselves grand homes on the flanks of Mont-Royale. At the turn of the nineteenth century it was claimed that the people who lived there – mostly of Scottish descent – controlled 70 per cent of the country's wealth.

The eyes of the Bridgeton boys were caught by the juxta-position of road names like St James Street (where the heirs of the Northwest Company fur-traders were still doing business) with the names of the ancient warehouses of the Ville St Marie. But it was not these so much as the number of taverns that excited the thirsty lads.

For the first time since their 'recruitment' as merchant seamen, the five found that in Montreal accommodation had actually been arranged for them. After being handed another week's wages, the men were given directions to the *Auberge du Vieux-Port* on rue de la Commune close to the harbour-side. A fine little hotel dating back to the 1880s with tall casement windows, rooms on five floors and comfortable brass beds, it was, the boys agreed, the best billet they had had so far. Their stay was to be one that the hard-pressed manager would never forget.

Some of the British seamen bound for Philadelphia were to be housed in even finer accommodation. Because of the large transient population in Montreal brought about by the war, a

126

number of them found themselves given rooms in some of the city's first-class hotels including *Le Chateau* on Sherbrooke Street. The huge, copper-roofed apartment building looked rather like a cross between a Scottish castle and a French Renaissance chateau; luckily for the shipping agents, the seamen placed there generally behaved rather better than their compatriots.

The first difference all the newcomers noticed was that the majority of the people in the city spoke French. They had, in fact, landed in the only French-speaking metropolis in North America and the second-largest French-speaking city in the world. Thankfully, the influx of immigrants over the years meant that English was widely understood, though not always appreciated by those proud of the ancient traditions.

Close to their hotel on rue de la Commune, the Bridgeton boys located Ben's, a bar run by a friendly Scots-Canadian, known simply as McTavish, who took to the free-spending Glasgow boys and filled them with plenty of booze and information about Montreal. Before his death some years ago, he was also a source of information about their exploits in the city.

Ben's was just one of hundreds of bars that had helped Montreal to gain a reputation as *the* place to be during the days of Prohibition in the thirties. It was then that hordes of thirsty Americans would pour over the border every weekend to drink and enjoy themselves. A good spot to find the action was rue St Denis and its adjacent streets where visitors and locals would down vast amounts of liquor and argue over politics, sport and religion until the early hours of the morning.

According to McTavish, very little had changed in the interim and the Bridgeton boys would have no trouble in finding great bars all across town. They could hardly believe their luck after Halifax – the mere mention of which caused the bar owner to chuckle loudly.

The gang also amused the owner with their skill at a local game of endeavouring to drink eight half-pints of beer without using their hands. The trick was to bend down, put your nose inside the glass and suck some of the beer into your mouth then grip the glass with your teeth, tilt it until all the beer had been drunk and put it back on the table. The boys won a number of bets with other customers until the night a man with false teeth removed his molars and used his gums to down all eight glasses in record time!

When the gang wanted to eat, McTavish recommended Mother Martin's, a delicatessen that specialised in hot, smoked meat sandwiches and T-bone steaks with French fries. They boys were all amused by the term 'French fries' and had to have it explained to them that this was just another word for 'chips'.

The bar owner even suggested that if they were going to be in the city for a time, they might like to visit the wrestling matches and striptease shows that were very popular with tourists. The gang took him at his word and saw a tag-team match at the Forum between two local heroes and a pair of Germans, and visited a strip show at the Gaiety which included a comedian, a male impersonator and a girl with dyed-blonde hair who stripped until she was naked except for a G-string and two tiny red flowers on her nipples.

Paddy Mulholland later told McTavish the thing that had stuck most in his mind about the performance: 'They *clatty* [dirty] auld fellas sittin' in the front row. When the lights went oop, they were ae sweatin' and buttonin' up their toosers. The dirty bleeders hae been wanking at the cow!'

When the laughter subsided, a conversation began among the group that none of them had been *gettin' oor hole* [having sexual intercourse] since they had left Glasgow. McTavish told the boys he knew where the prostitutes hung out, but on being told what the girls charged, they reckoned their rapidly diminishing funds would not run to such extravagances.

128

Out of the hearing of the bar owner, however, the gang discussed doing a little thieving. Perhaps they might try their luck in the big department stores they had heard about: *La Baie* round the corner in St Catherine's Street and Ogilvy's on the same road. Both proved too well guarded, although the boys did enjoy their visit to Ogilvy's, where a piper in a kilt was playing at the entrance and had to endure the ribald remarks of the genuine Scots from Glasgow.

McTavish was not, though, completely unaware of the intentions of his customers and later remembered how their eyes had lit up when he had told them about the Sun Life Building in the middle of town. This magnificent structure dominated the city's skyline and was for years the largest building in the British Commonwealth. A couple of security guards who worked there used the bar and had told McTavish in an unguarded moment that some of Britain's financial reserves and national treasures, which had been shipped out earlier in the war to avoid falling into the hands of the Germans in the event of an invasion, were now in the Sun Life vaults.

For all their bravado, the five Bridgeton boys knew they were not cut out to be bank robbers on that kind of scale. But they did dream up another scam, which McTavish remembered well.

The wages they were being paid were not enough to keep them in drink. So they set to work in their hotel. Despite the fact it was bitterly cold, they stripped their rooms of blankets and then threw them out of the side windows into the street late one night.

Then they stuffed them into bags and touted the blankets around the streets for five dollars. They were pretty good material and sold quickly. Within less than an hour, the gang were back at the hotel carrying bottles of whisky. No one seemed to notice anything was wrong!

According to McTavish, when the men had sold all their blankets, they began to surreptitiously strip the hotel of curtains, carpets and all manner of fittings:

Somehow they got out framed paintings from the rooms and solid brass bedroom door handles, as well as ash trays, hat stands, table lamps and even a lobby carpet. They took this stuff along to the Bonsecours Market where you could buy and sell anything. They were soon in funds again.

A still more extraordinary story is credited to the Bridgeton boys: that they stole a huge porcelain bath and used it to store a hoard of whisky. McTavish later recalled:

When the hotel had lost most of its furniture, the boys were forced to take jobs in a local shipyard. There they learned that by law, pay for 24 hours work could be claimed after just 14 hours had been worked. And they also discovered that this money could be paid in advance in an emergency.

So one of the boys phoned the shipyard's pay office and said that the ship they were sailing on was about to leave dock immediately and that they had to get paid off in full within the hour. The hoax worked and soon the boys were busy buying liquor by the case.

But, of course, they had nowhere to store it all and I'm told they poured it into a hotel bath. Then they wrenched the bath from its fittings, sealed it over, and carried it away with them into the night.

Incredible as it sounds, there is evidence that the Bridgeton boys were among those villains to blame for the stories that appeared in the *Montreal Matin* in December 1941 about an outbreak of lawlessness in the city. According to these reports, it was being claimed that mob rule had broken out in certain districts of the city.

The evidence points to the fact that other Glasgow gang members who had been released that autumn from Barlinnie, or 'recruited' from the city's underworld, to serve as merchant seaman, were also committing crimes of theft and robbery as well as threatening violence to the stallholders in the Bonsecours Market and a number of shopkeepers in the Chinatown district. Circumstantial details point to these gangsters having been a mixture of ex-cons and petty criminals from the Gorbals and Plantation districts as well as a few Bridgegate Boys from Gallowgate and perhaps two former Parlour Boys.

The first signs of trouble had been registered in the Chinatown area, an eighteen-block area of houses, shops and restaurants between rue René-Levesque and Avenue Vigar to the north and south and rue Hotel de Ville and rue Bleury on the west and east. The Chinese had settled in large numbers in the area after 1880 when the transcontinental railroad reached the city.

Although Montreal had at the time several other ethnic communities within its boundaries, the Chinese seemed particularly to attract the hostility of the Scotsmen and a series of disturbances and fights in the shops proved only a prelude to some serious attacks in which a number of the owners were taken to hospital for treatment for broken limbs and razor slashes. Though members of the families of the victims remained tight-lipped about the attackers, word in the community was that seamen with Scottish accents had been responsible.

The Bonsecours Market, created in 1845 as Montreal's main market selling primarily meat, fish and produce and retaining more than a vestige of its French inspiration, was also subjected to attacks on stallholders and demands for cash. Some of the intended victims had refused to hand over any money, but others had given in to weight of numbers when gangs of three, four or five men had threatened to wreck their business.

131

In the market, however, some of those who had been picked on were prepared to identify the villains to the police as strangers who spoke with strong Glasgow accents. Their accounts told of the hoodlums being armed with knives – and, especially, of the assured manner of their threats, indicating men practised in the art of intimidation.

When, as a result of these reports, the police stepped up patrols in Chinatown and the Bonsecours district, the criminals proved adept at avoiding arrest and disappearing in the narrow, winding streets of the adjacent districts. The market, in particular, located close to the harbour, was a warren of hiding places with which the men seemed to have familiarised themselves before commencing their criminal activities.

In a leader column devoted to these events under the head-line, 'Crime Wave', the *Montreal Matin* informed its readers:

Our city has always been welcoming to those from abroad and especially during times of war. At the moment, however, it seems we are hosting some criminal elements determined to create a private war of their own...The public at large can, we feel sure, take assurance that the forces of law and order in this city have never given in to mob rule and will not do so now even in difficult times.

With Christmas just a few days away, these were certainly heartening words. But there were still many among the citizens of Montreal – especially those in the troubled districts – who began to wonder just *when* the hardmen who were causing such problems might be moved on to fight in the real war? And if anyone outside the city was prepared to do anything about it...

Chapter 8

Trouble in the City of Brotherly Love

The longer the refitting of his new command, the *Catlin* – to be restored to its original name of the *George Washington* once this work was finished – went on in Philadelphia, the more concerned Captain David Bone became about both the ship and his crew. He had, in fact, every reason to feel this sense of apprehension, though there was as yet no precise information to back it up.

The decision to convert the old German liner into a troop transporter for the British had been arrived at solely between the United States Maritime Commissioners and the British Ministry of War Transport Department. The work on the ship was also completely under the control of Rear Admiral Watson and his naval engineers and shipyard workers on League Island and it is perhaps not surprising that Bone was beginning to feel rather like a kind of glorified clerk of works.

Still, the captain went down to the shipyards each day, trying not to give the impression that he wanted to interfere in the refitting, merely showing a keen interest in all that was going on. His weekly meetings with the American rear admiral were mostly amicable, but occasionally tense as the weeks of September rolled on into October. On each occasion, Watson would enquire when his officers and men were going to be relieved by a British crew.

David Bone had to use all his native Scottish tact to avoid being too specific – all the time remembering his instructions from London about the assignment. Several of his officers and leading crew members were, of course, already billeted in the city and spending as much time as they could on board the *Catlin* preparing themselves to take over the vessel, which was a comfort. Even so, before the liner would be able to put to sea as the *George Washington*, flying what would be her third national flag, the Red Ensign, at least 500 merchant seamen would be required to man her.

It was not until late in October, in fact, that Bone felt confident enough to report to Watson that sufficient men had safely crossed the Atlantic and were now in Canada for him to begin planning to bring them to the dockyard. However, he was concerned at the work these men would be required to do when they arrived, as he confided in his diary with considerable insight:

> What could be done at this stage of reconstruction with a mob of merchant seamen, doubtless softened and ill to organise after long shore-dwelling and an idle sea passage? It was not a good prospect and I felt that a major problem would arise if the Admiral insisted on his small maintenance party being immediately relieved.

Captain Bone felt the need to share this concern with Rear Admiral Watson. Another reason was the way in which discipline differed on particular types of British and American vessels. Bone had been informed that all American troop transporters were manned in much the same way as British armed merchant cruisers and their crews subject to naval discipline. However, he would not be running a regular naval ship and his men were all merchant seamen answerable only to the limited powers of the Merchant Shipping Acts under which they had signed on.

Fortunately, Rear Admiral Watson was quick to appreciate the discipline problems that might arise with such men let loose in a naval port. He was, though, still 'courteously impatient,' about wanting the new crew in situ, Bone noted – until fate came to the aid of the British commander in a most unexpected way.

It was the arrival at League Island of a badly damaged British destroyer, H.M.S. *Manchester*, commanded by Captain Harold Drew that provided the respite. The sleek-looking vessel had been extensively hit in an attack by a German U-boat, but had managed to limp her way across the Atlantic to Philadelphia. Now she was to undergo repairs, particularly on the flooded compartments where the bodies of some of her dead crew were still trapped, before returning to the fray.

Captain Bone was well aware of the acute shortage of accommodation in and around the dockyard that might be available for the *Manchester*'s crew while this work was carried out on the destroyer. But then a flash of inspiration gave him a solution that would ease the predicament of both the *Manchester*'s captain and himself. There was plenty of space on the *Catlin*. Why didn't the British sailors bunk there?

The idea was at once welcomed by Rear Admiral Watson, Captain Drew and especially the *Catlin*'s former captain, Lieutenant Jones, who was happy at last to be disembarking with his men. As the battle-weary English sailors from the destroyer tramped up the gangway, Bone allowed himself a wry smile at the thought of the unique situation in which he now found himself. He was a British merchant seaman in command of British naval officers berthed on a ship flying the US flag!

Work continued on the *Catlin* throughout the rest of October, and in November the vessel was moved to a dry dock for descaling. Bone was pleased at the state of the steel hull after it had been recoated, and felt that things were starting to come together when the vessel was returned to Pier 5. After completing the refurbishing of the troop decks and upper sections and the reinstatement of the name *George Washington* on the bow, the captain could contemplate going to sea again. Old 'Rip Van Winkle' really seemed to have been given a new lease of life.

On 28 November, Archie Roberts and his skeleton crew of stokers fuelled the bunkers and furnaces and fired the engines into life. This first trial did not involve the ship moving from the dockside, but as Bone watched the great shining cranks steadily revolve, his spirits began to rise. By the end of the first week of December, only the final welding on the boilers remained to be done.

But something unexpected occurred on the morning of Sunday, 7 December that accelerated the plans for the *George Washington* – the Japanese attack on Pearl Harbor which finally pushed the United States into the Second World War.

A telephone call from the British consul in Philadelphia awoke Captain Bone in his hotel room at the Wilton. When he lifted the receiver and heard from the diplomat what had happened, he realised at once that the merciless attack would affect his own plans. If the estimate of the number of US vessels that had been destroyed in the raid was true, then every available inch of space on League Island would be needed by the American Navy and he would probably be asked to leave with the *George Washington* as soon as possible.

And so it proved. Within 24 hours, Bone had been informed that the series of sea trials that were being arranged for the ship in Delaware Bay would have to be cancelled. The vessel had to be fuelled, provisioned and equipped as quickly as possible. She was to be ready for sea on 7 January and sail to New York to await further orders.

Bone spent a preoccupied and very busy Christmas with barely time to think about the festivities as he oversaw the work to make the *George Washington* ready for sea. He was, naturally, concerned at not being able to hold further trials. More worrying still was the fear that German U-boats, emboldened by this new turn of events, could well be hunting even closer to the American coast. A baptism of fire for his new command was not out of the question, he realised grimly.

But now, at last, he could give the orders for the remaining members of his crew to be summoned down from Canada to Philadelphia. And from the moment these men began to arrive at the US Navy Docks – a report was to state some years later – the ship, its captain and his officers were in trouble.

It is probably not stretching the truth too far to say that Philadelphia, despite its pioneer history and naval tradition, had rarely seen anything quite like a section of the *George Washington*'s crew who arrived in late December 1941. The city may have had a tradition among its male population of occasional lawlessness, a love of hard drinking and an admiration for those handy with their fists – in or out of the ring – but the Glasgow hardmen who strolled into town were the equal of almost any notorious citizen of the day. Or of the past, for that matter.

'The City of Brotherly Love', as Philadelphia was known because of its Quaker origins, exerted an immediate appeal for the gang for a number of reasons. The blend of the ancient and the modern – the historic public and ecclesiastical buildings, the slums on Eighth Street, the imposing residential section of Chestnut Hill, plus the bustling city centre – yet again reminded the boys of home. Indeed, none of them was surprised to learn that Scottish immigrants had played a part in the development of the sprawling city and that, like Glasgow, which depended on the Clyde, Philadelphia owed much of its prosperity to shipbuilding on the Delaware River.

Founded in 1682 as a Quaker colony by the Englishman, William Penn, the city had, a century later, become the birthplace of the nation and the centre of its first government – facts commemorated by Independence Hall and the famous Liberty Bell. Within a few years, Philadelphia was renowned as a port and industrial centre, famed for its metalworking, oil refining, textiles, printing and, of course, as a port and shipbuilding area. Now the fifth-largest city in the US, it had become well known, too, for its ethnic communities and the traces of their old cultures that these folk had brought with them from all over Europe.

It was not, though, a history lesson that the Bridgeton boys wanted when they left their train at the enormous Pennsylvania Railroad Station at Thirteenth and Market Street and headed between the fluted Corinthian columns of the exit and into the centre of town. The weather was bitterly cold and there was a blanket of snow over everything.

Shivering in the icy air, the boys were ready for a drink, and for somewhere that might offer fresh opportunities similar to those they had left behind in Montreal. Here, they hoped, the police would not yet be on the look-out for them.

The five men had already been given directions to the hotel where they were to stay – the Doans Hotel at the junction of Eighth Street and the bizarrely named Locust Street. According to the little map in John Wilson's hand, it was four blocks across the city beside Washington Square which the group could see signposted outside the station.

William McCormack was immediately intrigued by the name Doans as he had relatives back in Scotland with the same name. When the boys had checked into the hotel and were enjoying the first round of drinks served up by the talkative barman, they got to hear the legend of the five notorious brothers who had given their name to the establishment.

The Doans were members of a lowland Scots family who had become outlaws in Philadelphia during the early years of the nineteenth century. The five boys apparently objected to becoming involved in the War of Independence with England when it broke out in 1812 and were arrested for non-attendance on military duty. Heavily fined, their farm confiscated, the lads were now penniless, and as a contemporary report puts it:

> They resolved to follow the memorable examples of Dick Turpin and Claude Duval, and, taking to the road, became a terror to the whole countryside. Like their models, they were capriciously generous, giving freely to the poor what they stole from the rich; and the small farmers of the neighbourhood, whose political principles were of the vaguest order, had no fault to find with men who never took so much as a turnip from their fields, and who often assisted them in the profitable but perilous business of supplying food to the hungry English soldiers.

The five Scots laughed appreciatively at this ingenuity, though they all doubted whether they would have helped any Englishman. And, growing more relaxed and verbose as one drink followed another, they even began to suggest similarities between themselves and the Doans.

Bill Fullerton and Paddy Mulholland, who both had an eye for the girls, were also taken by another aspect of the Doan legend:

> Women, with their customary disregard for dull integrity, looked upon the five brothers as heroes of romance; while children, listening eagerly to tales of their intrepid exploits, resolved to be highwaymen themselves as soon as they were grown. There was no doubt that the Doans delighted to injure public property, but did no harm to the weak, the poor or the peaceful.

The barman explained that, inevitably, the local authorities had grown exasperated by this band of lawless Scots and a group of militiamen had been recruited to help the sheriff bring them to justice. The Doans, described in another account as 'strong, handsome, generous and humane', were finally cornered, and despite being heavily outnumbered put up a desperate resistance. Two were shot dead by the soldiers, another two captured, while the fifth managed to escape, never to be heard of again. The unfortunate pair of prisoners were taken to Philadelphia and, after a summary trial, hanged on the gallows in the High Street.

According to the Doans' barman, there was a lot of sympathy in the city for the brothers and a legend soon grew up around their bravery and kindness. Memories of their misdeeds faded and the outlaws came to be regarded as upholders of a lost cause rather than criminals who had been brought to justice. Thereafter they were assured a place in local folklore and were commemorated by the hotel which had carried their name for over a century.

That such a story should appeal to the Bridgeton boys was hardly surprising. Men who thumbed their noses at the law were very much to their liking. And that first night in Philadelphia, all of them went to bed convinced the place was going to suit them just fine.

In the days that followed, the group did, indeed, find that the cosmopolitan city, raucous with the sound of machinery and honking vehicles weaving through the crowded streets, had much to offer them. The hotel rooms, which cost a dollar a day, were perfect for the boys, too, though when their money did begin to run short they considered moving to one or other of the 25-cent 'flophouses' in the same neighbourhood

A few blocks from the hotel, just beyond the junction of Eighth and Arch Street, the boys discovered the 'tenderloin' district, which drew them like a magnet. Here amidst brash neon signs and burlesque posters, their noses were assailed by the smell of cheap restaurants, automats and hot-dog stands mingling with the unmistakable aroma of alcohol from numerous bars and taprooms.

The shabby apartment blocks, bawdy houses and missions were not unlike those back in Glasgow, and the stench of unwashed humanity and uncollected garbage was equally familiar. Some of the local people who watched the Scots from doorways and windows as they walked by had faces that mirrored their own expressions of defiance and hostility against the rest of the world.

The city's slums adjacent to the Delaware River were even more like the poorest streets in Bridgeton. One of these districts, bounded by Fifth and Race Street, was full of band-box houses and vermin-infested hovels, while another, between the inappropriately named Christian Street and Lombard, had a reputation for violence and drunkenness. In both, it was said, people's need for accommodation had been exploited to the utmost by ruthless landlords and burly, hard-faced debt collectors who were to be found on virtually every block.

The Glasgow boys had no intention of getting involved with the local hardmen in these districts. They themselves would have taken swift retribution on any Yanks muscling in on their territory, and, in any event, there were only five of them.

The same thoughts occurred to them when they walked to League Island. The route took them through the city's 'Little Italy' which stretched south from the Black section to the oil-covered flats of the Delaware River. The area teemed with humanity. Provalone cheeses dangled in the shop windows and the odour of red wine hung in the air. The five Scots walked warily – they all knew a little about the Mafia and were aware of sharp-eyed young men of Sicilian and Calabrian origin watching them as they passed along Ninth Street and Wharton, carefully avoiding rows of push-carts laden with fish, meat and vegetables lined up on both sides of the road.

On the west bank of the Delaware, in a taproom with views across the piers, wharfs and warehouses, the group supped beers and discussed their prospects. Straddling the river was a huge suspension bridge linking the city with Camden, New Jersey; in its shadow tugs, barges and freighters moved in an endless procession, loading and unloading cargoes. Beyond the blocks of houses stood some gigantic oil refineries and the navy yard where their ship, the *George Washington*, was being made ready to sail.

The thought of working as stokers did not fill them with pleasure. Hard work was something to be avoided at any cost – and they had done pretty well so far. It was time for a last binge or two before they were rounded up for sailing.

The group found echoes of the Halifax liquor laws in those of Philadelphia, which had been explained to them by the friendly barman in Doans. The early Scotch and Irish whisky distillers in Pennsylvania had, apparently, for years ignored or opposed the excise law, and had gone so far on several occasions as to 'tar and feather' those tax collectors who tried to make the system work. In the end, the patience of the government had run out and an army of 15,000 men was sent into the state to deal with the manufacturers.

Later, during the era of Prohibition, bootleg liquor, speakeasies and gangsters had sprouted like fungi in the city, resulting in an intensive drive by the Philadelphia police against organised crime. Then, with the repeal of Prohibition, the first state liquor stores were opened in the city in 1934.

Beer, whisky, wine – liquor in general – could be drunk in any of the bars or restaurants in the city. But because the sale of all spirits was a state monopoly, alcohol could be bought only at liquor stores run by the Pennsylvania Liquor Control Board; it was purchased in sealed containers marked 'Not To Be Opened On The Premises'. Although these stores were open from 10 a.m. to 9 p.m. on weekdays, they were closed all day on Sunday. The Bridgeton boys were not keen on the idea of dry Sundays.

It did not take them long to find where these liquor stores were located, or to plan what to do. The biggest were on Walnut, Sansom, Chestnut and Arch Streets, and in a concerted series of dips – much like the ones they had pulled at off-licences in Glasgow – the boys lifted two or three bottles from each in the course of a single day.

Three of Philadelphia's department stores also received their attention: Wannamaker's by City Hall, Snellenburg's two blocks down on Market Street, and the pair of adjacent buildings run by Gimbel Brothers right in front of the Federal Courts Building on Ninth Street. Delighted at their haul, the gang could only smile at the courtesy they received in all the shops from assistants anxious to make the 'limey seamen' feel welcome. Then they had robbed the places blind.

The shoppers who poured into the city as Christmas neared only made it easier for the Glasgow boys in their multifarious activities. They picked pockets in another store, Frank & Seders, and were just as lucky in the jewellery district on Sansom Street where the huddles of dealers at the 'curb market' were quite unaware of their wallets being removed while they bargained over little bags of gems.

The gang were less fortunate, though, at a number of the cheaper shops on South and Bainbridge Streets, also packed with seasonal bargain hunters. Here it seemed people were keeping a much tighter hold on their valuables as if being made uneasy by the *schleppers*, or barkers, outside the premises trying to buttonhole customers to go inside. Their patter reminded the boys of some of the con artists who tried the same tricks in Glasgow.

The Philadelphia police, under pressure to keep the festive mass of people and traffic moving, received reports of the thefts and an outbreak of pickpocketing, but according to reports in the *Evening Public Ledger* suspected either local villains or outsiders from New York. In the meantime, the boys from Bridgeton and some of the other ex-con 'recruits' continued their rip-roaring way through the city.

The first day of January 1942 was a red-letter day for all the merchant seamen in Philadelphia as well as the citizens themselves, with the holding of the Mummers' Parade. Christmas had been fun for everyone, but the New Year's Day celebrations were a riot.

The parade, which had originated on the opening day of 1901 to mark the new century, was actually based on a much more ancient British tradition. The ancestor of the celebration was a 'Saturnalia' held under the auspices of the 'Lord of Misrule', a fantasy figure known to the Scots as the 'Abbot of Unreason'. To the Bridgeton boys it was a night for getting well and truly bevvied in an orgy of boozing.

In fact, the parade, which had become as much an integral part of the city's calendar as Mardi Gras in New Orleans, had started out as an event lasting from Christmas week to the New Year, when brightly costumed groups of 'mummers' went around the streets of Philadelphia explaining the meaning of their strange dress in return for donations to charity. These costumes had all been prepared by local people and clubs during the preceding year and the best were awarded prizes by various civic and business associations.

The event climaxed on New Year's Day with all the mummers parading their elaborate headgear, huge capes and dazzling costumes along Broad Street, the city's great thoroughfare. Accompanying them were elaborately decorated floats, marching bands, and various groups burlesquing contemporary events and prominent people. Along the sidewalks, hundreds of thousands of spectators joined in the fun.

The week-long festivities had, however, been cut back to a single day after tragedies in successive years when a number of people had caught pneumonia because of exposure to the cold in their flimsy costumes. An attempt to switch the parade to the spring or summer had caused uproar among the traditionalists and a compromise was reached in 1935 with an agreement to restrict the mummers to just one day. The year after this decision, over a million people had thronged the streets in a riot of colour and noise.

1 January 1942 also produced one of the best Mummers' Parades, despite the anxiety many people were feeling in the aftermath of the declaration of war. The costumes were, if anything, more colourful and outrageous than before and among the figures being burlesqued were Hitler and several of his Nazi henchmen.

In the midst of the clamour and excitement, the seamen destined for the *George Washington* moved from bar to bar along Broad Street spending their ill-gotten gains. In many of these they were warmly greeted by Philadelphians who encouraged them to 'go and give those damn Nazis a hammering'.

The five Bridgeton boys fell into one bar on Eighth and Lehigh Street, unaware that they were in a predominantly German neighbourhood. Ever since the end of the First World War, groups of refugees from Germany had come to settle in Philadelphia, and a wave of immigrants had arrived when Hitler became *Reichsführer*. Now peacefully integrated into the city and celebrating the Mummers' Parade in their own way, the men and women at the tables had not expected to be invaded by a party of drunken Scotsmen.

Realising from the conversations that they were among Germans, Wilson and McCormack, by far the drunkest of the gang, began to hurl abuse at the customers about Hitler and threaten a fight. Tempers started to fray and when even the offer of drinks did nothing to defuse the situation, the proprietor decided to telephone the police.

Two officers who happened to be patrolling the vicinity arrived within minutes and, showing remarkable understanding, herded the five Scotsmen out and pointed them in the direction of the Doans Hotel. The officers did, though, remain on the sidewalk until the shambling group, some clinging to each other, disappeared into the first traces of dawn.

It had been a hell of a night – and it would be a hell of week for the men's new commander, Captain Bone, as he wrestled to establish order from all the disorder surrounding him.

As the merchant seamen who had been signed on in Glasgow to crew the *George Washington* began to arrive at the ship in various states of disarray and intoxication, stories of their exploits started to circulate among the regular crew members and ship's officers. In time, they reached the ears of Captain Bone, too.

He had, of course, been expecting problems with some of the men on the loose for so long with nothing to do. But while the tales he heard were mostly of drunkenness and the occasional fight, some were more worrying. He wrote in his diary:

The men were in funds. I learned that many had sought outside employment in Canada whilst awaiting the manning of the ship. They had found that employment profitable, but the effect of such uncommon riches – a manna from strange gods, with the convenience of a great city in which to consume it – taxed the patience of the ship's officers in the busiest days of reconversion. Although Rear Admiral Watson's thought of disorder was not seriously confirmed by the dockyard guard, there were incidents and anxious moments.

In the main these incidents consisted of the US Navy's patrol wagon arriving at the ship's gangway with hung-over and occasionally truculent seaman. To begin with, Bone found it hard to convince the marine guards that he had no legal powers to restrain and punish merchant seamen when they went out on the town and fell to behaving badly.

Rumours also reached the captain about the far worse behaviour of some of the Glasgow recruits. Bone had by now learned from sources in the Anchor Line about the virtual press-ganging of some of these men. With all the other demands on his time, he could only hope that his experienced officers and leading seamen would be able to handle even the toughest of them.

Once the majority of the 500-strong crew were gathered on the ship, the conditions on board prompted the first rumblings of discontent, not just from those like the Glasgow boys who had never sailed before, but also from veterans of many transatlantic voyages.

Because the *George Washington* was a coal-burning vessel, a core of seamen with experience of stoking had been assembled by Archie Roberts to man the furnaces. Their numbers were to be augmented by men with the least experience of merchant shipping but with, it was hoped, the strongest muscles. Under the authority of the no-nonsense Roberts it was believed they would knuckle down to life in the stokehold.

However, as Captain Bone was soon to observe, even the most experienced stokers had never before worked in such a labyrinth of bunkers and mammoth boilers as they now found in the old German liner. To be sure, electrical conveyors had been installed to bring the coal from the most distant bunkers, but that still left an awful lot of shovelling if the men were to keep the ship's engines in steam and up to pressure.

The Glasgow hoodlums were, frankly, horrified when they got their first sight of where they were to work. In fact, their sullen looks almost matched those of the regulars as the two groups sized each other up. Both knew they would have to try to get on, and they were at least united in their dislike of the conditions.

Up on the bridge, Captain Bone consulted with his officers. His message was brief and to the point. He warned them all that as soon as the *George Washington* left port it might be as hard to keep the pressure of the vessel's boilers *up* as to keep that of some of the men *down*.

Chapter 9

Mutiny on the
George Washington

The log of the *George Washington* records that the British Merchant Service took over the ship under the Lend-Lease Agreement on 29 September 1941 and that the partly refurbished vessel sailed from Philadelphia on the morning of 10 January 1942, her premature departure necessitated by the attack on the US fleet in Pearl Harbor and the need of the American Navy for wharf space in the League Island yards.

These notes do not mention that it was a bright, clear day, intensely cold. All around Pier 5 was a mass of grinding sheets of ice and the iron-grey vessel had to be towed out by a tug into the middle of the Delaware River to begin her voyage. Nor do they state that among the crew of 500 were a number of hung-over 'recruits' from the toughest section of Glasgow, ill-prepared to stoke the ship for her journey to New York.

In the stokehold, these men were being urged to 'gae their backs intae it' by the leading stoker, Archie Roberts, assisted by four merchant seamen he had sailed with before and who were more than ready to go through hell for the old man. Tough and resilient themselves, these stokers were not about to be fazed by some fractious ex-cons.

Wilson, McCormack, Fullerton, McCourt and Mulholland had made no secret of their past. If they hoped to intimidate the stokers, they signally failed because these were men who knew their safety at sea depended on looking after the boilers and engines. They sensed that their hasty exit from port meant the old liner's machinery was probably not entirely reliable, and they were not going to get distracted by a bunch of so-called *gemmies* [hardmen].

If the Glasgow boys did not set to it, the old hands had decided among themselves, then they would feel someone's knuckles or the back of a shovel. Lines were drawn and each group of men watched the other warily as they shovelled the coal into the roaring furnace.

The ship's captain, David Bone, knew all about the frictions that could develop among seamen at the start of a voyage, but he was somewhat surprised at the extent of the simmering anger in the stokehold. Archie Roberts, however, believed he could handle the situation. The two long-serving merchant seamen looked each other in the eyes, acknowledged how things *might* be without the need of words, and then the leading stoker returned below decks.

The *George Washington* slowly crunched its way through the ice downstream towards the Delaware Capes and the sea beyond. The 93-mile route would take her past the cities of Chester and Wilmington, by the towns of Dover and Milford on the southern bank, and finally between the Capes of Henlopen and May into the open Atlantic waters.

If the captain knew of any significance about a town by the name of Bridgeton, which the ship passed on the river's northern bank, he gave no indication to his officers. But in the stokehold, when this extraordinary coincidence was pointed out to the Glasgow boys, sweating in the glow of the ship's furnaces, William McCormack muttered that he 'fooking well knew where I would rather be'.

Years of experience had led Captain Bone to take as many precautions as possible to avoid trouble with either the ship or the crew. As he noted in his diary, 'We shall be taking many elements of potential disaster to sea with us and I have consulted with fellow officers for solutions.'

With the agreement of Rear Admiral Watson, for the first leg of the voyage to New York he took on board a group of workers from the League Island dockyards. Among these were three overseers, six foremen and a working squad of several dozen men whose knowledge of the boat from refitting her, he estimated, should be enough to deal quickly with any technical or engineering problems that might occur.

A discussion with Captain Drew, the commander of the destroyer H.M.S. *Manchester*, provided Bone with the answer to another potentially tricky situation. With his ship being repaired and some of his men idle, Drew agreed to draft a group of his engineering room crew to the *George Washington* to add a little experience and muscle below decks.

Bone made it clear that he wanted these men to act not as an armed guard over his unskilled stokehold recruits – that, he knew, would be confrontational and would only make any bad feelings worse – but as a stand-by team who could step into the breach if skilled hands were suddenly needed. He would have reason to be glad of this decision.

Yet despite the unobtrusive way in which these Navy men were brought on board, the merchant seamen soon guessed their purpose. The gossip that reached the stokehold – inevitably distorted in the retelling – did not help the attitude of the Glasgow 'recruits' who now had another focus for their objections. Indeed, it seems probable that the presence of these men influenced another piece of talk that reached the captain's ear and which he later committed to his notes about the voyage:

For some days I pondered a rumour that was current below decks that the ship would not be 'fired' beyond the Delaware Capes. Most commanding sailors are accustomed to crossing unfamiliar bridges at the first approach and are allergic to hearsay, but this seemed a possibility. Although nothing occurred, I was happy and grateful to have the men from the *Manchester* on board.

Another report of this journey to New York describes Captain Bone as 'sitting on a time bomb that could explode at any moment'. On board the *George Washington*, it said, he had some hoodlum crew members who were 'glad to be getting away from a city that was becoming too hot for them'.

A more worrying *fact* was conveyed to the captain by the chief engineer even before the *George Washington* reached the Capes. He informed Bone that one of the boilers was already showing the first signs of over-strain. It was not bad enough to cause concern *yet*, but all the officers on the bridge shared their commander's feeling that the news was ominous.

As the vessel steamed along the long river passage to the sea, it became evident that it would not move at a sufficient speed until a number of adjustments and alterations had been carried out. So at a point on the navigation map marked as Ship John Shoal, Captain Bone stopped and dropped anchor. An examination of the engines revealed that the bearings had overheated and would take the maintenance crew several hours to fix. By the time this work was complete, the *George Washington* had missed the tide and had to remain at anchor until daylight.

The stop had, though, been welcomed in the stokehold. The Bridgeton boys were laid off duty and told to get some rest. Instead, it seems, they pulled out from under their bunks several bottles of whisky that they had smuggled on board, and subsequently all fell into a drunken sleep. At least it enabled them to forget for a few hours that they were about to enter the open sea where U-boats could well be lying in wait.

The next day saw the *George Washington* pass by Cape Henry and out into the open Atlantic. There was very little wind and

Captain Bone felt there was a good chance that the conditions might remain fair long enough to make good time on the remaining 150-mile voyage to New York. He hoped so, at least.

As he had done many times since the outbreak of the war, the captain took out his binoculars and began to scan the ocean for any signs of the enemy. A briefing from the British consul's office in Philadelphia before leaving the port had brought him up to date on German activities off the coast of America. But when dealing with such a cunning adversary, even the best information was not always correct. For example, no one seemed quite sure whether the Germans, or the Americans for that matter, had laid any minefields along this vulnerable stretch of coast.

It did seem evident, however, that long-range U-boats were operating in the territorial waters between Maine and Florida. Their first targets had been the lumbering oil tankers travelling up from the Gulf of Mexico to the northern cities, and these attacks had been followed by others on troop transporters – a fact that made Bone understandably nervous.

The United States had not been long in the war in January 1942, and the government had not yet properly organised the civilian and military precautions necessary to combat an enemy who struck efficiently, often under the cover of darkness and with increasingly successful results. Many of the towns along the Atlantic seaboard had not yet dimmed their lights, as the people of Britain had done, in order to make it harder for German attackers to see their targets. The fact that lights still shone out from the coastal towns and ports also silhouetted vessels passing near land and made them easy pickings for the lurking U-boats.

As Captain Bone prepared to sail north along the coast of New Jersey, no blackout regulations were in force and the plans for a convoy system with groups of boats protected by US Navy destroyers and cruisers were still at the discussion stage.

He had not even been given a specific route to make his solitary way to New York and the only crumb of comfort he had been offered was the fact that there were supposed to be a number of air patrols operating along the coast.

Unlike his previous commands, though, the *George Washington* was armed. Six guns were strategically placed along the main deck and the ship carried qualified gunners with experience of the Battle of the Atlantic. They would certainly be useful if any aerial attacks were made.

The *George Washington* also had several surface weapons intended to be used against U-boats. But there was a problem – all were British-made and in the haste of leaving League Island, Rear Admiral Watson's men had been unable to obtain any ammunition.

Despite all these concerns, Captain Bone was still determined to use the voyage to New York to carry out the trials that shortage of time had prevented him from undertaking on the Delaware River. He sent a message down to Archie Roberts in the stokehold to prepare his men for speed tests.

The account of these trials that was subsequently logged with the *George Washington*'s papers indicates that 'erratic and unskilful firing' generated an average speed of about nine knots during the morning exercise, and this could be increased to no better than thirteen knots in the afternoon. The words 'erratic and unskilful' are open to different interpretations. It has been suggested that the reason for this was that the stokers were still new to the job; another version, emanating from the Bridgeton boys, was that they deliberately worked slower despite all Archie Roberts' cursing and threats. Whatever the truth, the results left the officers of the *George Washington* far from happy.

Just as these trials ended on a stretch of the sea not far from Atlantic City, something most unexpected hove into view. The sea was then completely empty of any other shipping and there was no sign of any U-boat activity. It was a giant US Coastguard airship that slowly crossed the skyline until it was over the ship.

The officers of the ship, who might have expected a patrolling warship or even a spotter plane, were completely taken aback by the sight of the great, grey ellipsoid. High above them, the crew of the airship were looking down in similar amazement. The erratic behaviour of the *George Washington* while undergoing her trials, compounded by problems with the steering gear, had made the vessel look for all the world like a ship out of control. And the fact she was flying the unfamiliar Red Ensign had heightened the confusion and brought out the coastguard airship to investigate.

On the bridge, Captain Bone received a call from the airship to identify himself. He replied promptly with the ship's name, the port from which she had come and her destination of New York. The silence on the radio grew pregnant with suspense as minutes passed by. Then came a request to repeat the particulars.

An officer standing next to the captain suddenly realised what had happened. The name *George Washington* had probably not yet been widely circulated – indeed it might still be struck off from earlier days when she had been taken out of service. The information was repeated with the additional fact that the ship was 'ex-USS *Catlin*'. This time the response was quicker and in the affirmative. It is difficult to guess which of the two parties was more relieved!

A further message was sent to the airship requesting information on any U-boats reported in the vicinity. The negative reply was warmly welcomed on the bridge as the airship turned majestically and headed back to the shore, leaving the *George Washington* to continue on her journey north.

The difficulties the vessel was experiencing did not end with the sea trials, however. According to the ship's log the boilers which had been water-tested at League Island, were now showing new weaknesses when actually working at sea, while the hydraulic system that controlled the water-tight bulkhead doors was not functioning correctly. Far more worrying than either of these was the fact that a valve had fractured in the forward stokehold and the area was now awash with sea-water.

The veteran stokers in the hold had seen this sort of thing before and were not unduly worried. The fault was reported to the bridge by Archie Roberts and he was immediately promised a gang of the American dockyard workers to patch the valve. The Bridgeton boys, however, tired, thirsty and exhausted by their labours, were in an even blacker mood than usual and busy convincing themselves that 'the bloody auld tub is sinking'.

That night, when the group fell into their bunks at the end of their shift, they were more than just angry at Archie Roberts and the other stokers, even the officers and the *George Washington* itself. What they had in mind was mutiny.

Captain Bone had a growing feeling that the men below decks were getting ever more restless. He had experience of the signs, of course, and had already written in his diary for 12 January 1942: 'After we passed the Capes, I learned that the voice of authentic Clydeside in the stokeholds and bunkers, though still mutinous and threatening, was not yet definitely pitched to active revolt.'

If he had been privy to the conversation that went on the following night among the Bridgeton boys he might not have been so sure of himself. The evidence is that the group actually began to plan a mutiny with the intention of taking over the ship and forcing the captain to sail them to a neutral port. There they would abandon ship and carry on their free-spirited lifestyle until the war was over.

Among those who remembered this event on the *George Washington* was John Burgess, a steward who lived until the time of his death in Wandsworth, London. He talked about his experiences in the late fifties:

> I've never forgotten that tough section of Glasgow boys in the stokehold. They got up to such mischief that it reflected on us all. They were always looking for ways to get out of work and when they were drunk they were a real menace. They hated life on the ship and it was only the fact the other stokers were as tough as them prevented more trouble.

Burgess, who among his duties served in the canteen where the boys ate, remembered overhearing a conversation that was obviously part of an ongoing plan. The hoodlums knew they would be in New York before long and reckoned if they were going to do anything it had to be soon:

> What they wanted to do was round up all the disgruntled seamen who had been forced into signing up for the *George Washington*, grab some weapons from the armoury, and take Captain Bone a prisoner. They would then force him to turn the ship around and sail to South America. Somewhere like Port of Spain or Georgetown. There they planned to head for the countryside and hide out until after the war was over.

The situation looked ugly to Burgess and he wondered just how much the captain knew about the unrest. It would be very dangerous for everyone if the men got hold of any guns, even if they collected up some of the blunt instruments from the stokehold, and the steward was debating whether to tell the chief steward what he had heard, when events took their own course:

> That night I was woken up in my cabin by sounds of a commotion coming from the bar. I went along there and

found two of the ship's officers and some of the men from H.M.S. *Manchester* in a furious argument with a group of the Scots. They had obviously broken into the bar and were all at least three sheets to the wind. Fists began to fly and for a minute it looked like the Glasgow boys were getting the upper hand. I remember one of them shouting, 'We'll soart ye out and show ye how to run this fooking ship ye *bam-pots.*'

As I was standing in the doorway wondering what the hell to do, Captain Bone suddenly appeared and stormed into the room. You should have seen him lay into those Scots boys. He stopped them dead in their tracks. They might have been prepared to take on the others, but they were no match for the 'Old Man'.

The captain hadn't earned his nickname of 'The Brass-bounder' for nothing. He was as tough as nails and certainly didn't seem afraid of the Scottish hoodlums who we all knew had a reputation for fighting and carrying knives. Anyway, when he'd finished lambasting them, they cleared up the bar like lambs and then headed off back to their bunks. That was the last time I heard any talk of mutiny.

Captain Bone himself referred to this incident only obliquely in a note he wrote later to Captain Drew of the *Manchester* thanking him for the loan of his men:

It was not considered vitally necessary or indeed politic to employ them in the stokehold on the passage from Philadelphia. At times there was a sore temptation to do so: but there was always the tempering thought that the crew we had signed on our Articles of Agreement were the men – good, bad, or indifferent – with whom we would have to live and work for months to come. It seems certain, though, that the *moral support* [author's italics] of the presence on board of naval stokers imposed a curb on our 'hotheads' and for that I am grateful to you.

John Burgess, for his part, always believed that it was the intervention of the unyielding captain that was most responsible for putting a stop to the Glasgow boys' plan for a takeover of the ship. But it would not be their last act of defiance by any means.

Seemingly putting the scenes of rebellion out of his mind, Captain Bone pressed on with the ship's journey to New York. Following all the setbacks, his optimism was growing. Although the *George Washington* continued to prove herself far from the easiest ship to navigate, she was still perhaps capable of fulfilling her mission. The dockyard technicians continued to remedy the problems as they arose, and those faults that were only temporarily repaired were marked down for more careful attention once the vessel reached harbour.

The whole time, however, the officers and crew kept a wary eye out for any signs of submarine activity. Captain Bone tried to calm fears with his own, slightly tongue-in-cheek theory, that the ship's erratic progress and the appearance of the coastguard airship could have been confusing, if not actually offputting, to any U-boat commander observing her. Perhaps, he argued, the enemy might have come to the conclusion that the vessel was a new type of 'Q Ship' and best avoided. In any event, no submarine came near.

Before the *George Washington* reached New York, the increasing faith that Bone had been putting in her was rewarded when a north-east gale suddenly blew up. In minutes, the old liner was ploughing head-on into mounting seas and the captain realised in that moment just why she had remained in service for so long across the Atlantic. He wrote in his journal:

The ship exhibited good temper in the rising gale by the way she 'shouldered' the seas and, even at such a slow speed, displayed a surprising response to helm action. To a certain degree, I had anticipated that her great length and the curious old-fashioned sternward projection of her propellers might promote an ease of handling, but I had not guessed at her sea kindliness in adverse weather. For that alone I warmed towards her.

Below decks in the stokehold, the Bridgeton boys were feeling anything but warmly inclined towards the ship. The sudden onset of the heaving seas had made two of them violently sick, and two were clutching their stomachs. Only Paddy Mulholland seemed to weather the storm. Around them, the experienced merchant seamen enjoyed the Glaswegians' discomfort and cursed them for the landlubbers they were.

Things did not improve as the ship passed Ocean Port and Rumson and the lookout began to search for signs of Long Island and New York on the horizon. In fact a snowstorm had now blown up to add to the churning water of the Atlantic, and the *George Washington* had to slow even her snail's pace for the last few miles. The discomfort continued for the men below decks until the ship was finally anchored off Staten Island on the morning of 16 January.

It would be 24 hours before the five Glaswegians had the stomach for tackling the pleasures of New York. In the meantime, all the other crew members had disembarked from the ship and been ferried to the South Ferry terminal to be let loose on Manhattan.

The Bridgeton boys were still sore at the way they had capitulated to Captain David Bone and were nursing thoughts of revenge. When they took stock and realised how little money they had for booze in their new port of call, an idea occurred to them. They knew that an army of mechanics and fitters would

160

soon be swarming all over the *George Washington* putting her right before the next stage of her voyage. So why didn't they help themselves to a few things that could be sold to raise cash?

The steward, John Burgess, who had already gone ashore, would be the person to discover the theft because a number of the items were removed from the bar and canteen where he worked. Although he did not witness the event, he said there was no one else left on the ship who might have taken the ornate items and gold fitments that had been on the ship ever since its glory days of transatlantic travel.

Unfortunately for Wilson, McCormack, Fullerton, McCourt and Mulholland, the ship's supply of alcohol was safely under lock and key in the bond, so they had to make do with the fittings, which they hid in their overcoats before waiting for a ferry to take them ashore. The three crew members left on board to await the arrival of the repairers were in no hurry to summon a ferry for the bunch of malcontents. Until, that is, a hint of physical violence stirred them into action. If the men had any suspicion about the bulky objects under the Scotsmen's clothes they certainly did not have the courage to say so.

Riding across the Upper Bay from the *George Washington*, the shivering group gave barely a second glance to the Statue of Liberty and were more interested in the welcoming lights on the shore. The skyscrapers thrusting into the darkened heavens were being dusted with snow and the men could see that a blanket of snow had covered the Lower West Side of Manhattan. Once the ferry docked, they had only one thought – making up for lost time in the city's myriad bars. And they would be glad to get out of the perishing cold.

The next few days were a long round of drinking as the Glasgow hardmen worked their way through the bars from the lower end of Broadway around City Hall up to Central Park and the outskirts of the Bronx. Thereafter they began retracing their steps and had one rip-roaring all-night session in a bar on Forty-Second Street. In this road, famous for its vice dens and pornography shops, the gang made friends with some small-time New York criminals.

William McCormack and Bobbie McCourt were fascinated by the hoodlums' stories of life in New York. The Big Apple was a place of easy pickings, they were told: it was easy to get a girl to prostitute herself for you, and when money got short there were always crime bosses who needed little jobs taking care of. America might be at war, but there was no stopping crime, and smart guys kept well away from recruiting stations. Why risk your ass when you could have a good time in NY?

Before the night was out, McCormack and McCourt had agreed to join the local mobsters. They were going to desert the ship. The others could go back to stoking the hellhole if they liked, but there was nothing for them back in Glasgow – only that bastard Robinson and his *busies* – so why not start a new life here?

Perhaps it was the drink talking? But when the other three Bridgeton boys awoke from sleeping off their hangovers the next day, there was no sign of McCormack or McCourt. For a while the trio sat in silence looking out at the snow-covered panorama of New York wondering if they – or the other two – had made the right decision.

The records of those crew members who sailed in the *George Washington* indicate that McCormack and McCourt did not, indeed, report back for duty and they were duly listed as missing. The details were eventually forwarded to the authorities in Glasgow in case the men should return there. No trace of either man, though, or even what lives they pursued, has ever been found.

In the intervening period, Captain Bone had been occupied on quite different matters. Immediately after docking he had sought out the local director of the British Ministry of War Transport, Philip Rees, to report the problems with his ship and arrange the repairs that would need to be carried out before he could continue on the next stage of his journey to Halifax to take on board troops for England.

With commendable speed, Rees made arrangements for the *George Washington* to be repaired by a local mercantile firm, Bethlehem Shipyards Inc. With this arrangement in place, the technicians and mechanics from League Island could be released to return to Philadelphia along with the crewmen from H.M.S. *Manchester*.

Two days later, the liner was steamed into one of Bethlehem Shipyards' berths at Chelsea Pier and work began at once in the boiler and engine rooms. When Captain Bone went aboard to meet the repair crew, he was delighted to hear from one man that the company actually had a long association with his ship. One or other of their piers on the west side of the Hudson River had regularly serviced the ship ever since her maiden voyage for the North German Lloyd Line from Bremerhaven to New York back in 1909. They had also been responsible for repairing the damage after the sabotage attempt by her crew in 1917, and continued this work when ownership passed to the United States Lines in 1921.

For a number of the Bethlehem workers it was like dealing with an old friend. They were familiar with the engines and power systems and their long-term knowledge of the quirks of the ship was of great comfort to Captain Bone. Meeting the foreman boiler-maker was even more encouraging as the man claimed to know every rivet of her boilers.

The commander was able to leave the *George Washington* in capable hands and enjoy some welcome relaxation in New York before the next stage of the saga. This gave him time for some more thoughts about his crew. They had been on shore for some time and the number of tasks for them to attend to was already mounting up. When the men began to return there were quite a number under the weather, as Bone noted in his diary:

There have been difficulties once again. The waterfront saloons near the Chelsea Piers are singularly convenient for a quick 'warmer' in working hours – but indiscipline was no more than was to be expected in the early imposition of ship routine.

More particularly, though, he was concerned about the men in the engine room. Especially those, whom he did not name, though there can be little doubt as to whom he was referring, he called 'the many incompetents in the stokeholds'. In consultation with Archie Roberts, Bone decided to transfer these men to other duties. Once they were at the mercy of the elements and German submarines on the Atlantic Ocean, he said, it would be essential to maintain steam at a constant rate. There could be no more erratic and unskilful stoking of the *George Washington*.

When the three remaining members of the Bridgeton boys dragged themselves back to the ship, the news that they were being moved out of the stokehold was greeted with delight and a series of V-signs at the regular stokers as they trio disappeared in the direction of their cabins. Whatever they were given to do had to be better than heaving coal.

They might even, John Wilson suggested as they swallowed their first drinks that night, have the time to make some new plans before it was too late to avoid the God-awful trip back across the Atlantic?

Chapter 10

Finale at 'Torpedo Junction'

After just over two weeks of intensive work in the Bethlehem Shipyards, the *George Washington* was judged seaworthy and ready for the next part of her journey to Halifax, where she was scheduled to pick up 4,000 troops for transportation to Britain. As Captain David Bone entered the navigation bridge once again to start the voyage, he looked out at a harbour that he had sailed in and out of on numerous occasions.

In truth, he could not at that moment remember the number of times he had seen the welcoming beacon of the Ambrose Lightship marking the sea-gate to the Port of New York. The difference on this occasion was that America was no longer neutral but at war, and the density of the shipping in the vicinity was an immediate sign of the changed circumstances.

Notable among this armada was a group of fifteen deeply laden merchantmen all streaked in amazing patterns of camouflage. They were evidently preparing to sail in convoy across the Atlantic. Riding at anchor nearby were three sleek US warships, which Captain Bone looked at admiringly.

The *George Washington*'s journey up the eastern seaboard was to be made alone, without the benefit of any kind of escort despite the increased threat from U-boats now that the US was directly involved in the conflict. First, the captain steamed her up to a position just south of Fire Island and, with the wide Atlantic ahead, he set a course to the north. As he did so, Bone was able to comfort himself with the knowledge that his vessel was now *fully* armed. He noted this fact in the ship's log:

> We can now fight back against any attack. Ammunition has been taken on at the powder anchorage before sailing. Paravanes, which are our protection against moored mines, have been streamed and approved. With the Degauss installation we have to rely upon the scientific accuracy of its designer for there was no testing range available to us in western waters.

The log indicates that during the voyage to Halifax the ship's defensive equipment was exercised on several occasions. As a result, Captain Bone felt confident about the ability of his gunners to give a good account of themselves in the eventuality of the vessel being attacked during the Atlantic crossing. He was less satisfied, though, with the efforts being made by some of the new recruits to the deck crew.

Captain Bone's decision to reallocate the 'incompetents' from the stokeholds to lesser duties had enabled Archie Roberts to supervise the training of the remaining men. This, in turn, had produced an overall improvement in maintaining the vessel's steam. Indeed, the *George Washington* was able to make a steady speed of fourteen knots all the way from New York to Halifax.

The three remaining Bridgeton hoodlums – Wilson, Fullerton and Mulholland – undoubtedly found their new jobs as general hands less taxing than heaving coal in the fiery boiler room. But this did not prevent them from getting into trouble with other crew members. Bill Fullerton, in particular, had become increasingly truculent and on the first night at sea got himself involved in a brawl over a pin-up picture.

The stopover in New York had enabled the more literate crew members to replenish their supplies of magazines and books. The lurid covers of some of the paperbacks, showing semi-naked women, gave a clear indication of the men's tastes. One particular title, *It Happened One Night*, with an illustration of the exotic French-born *femme fatale*, Claudette Colbert, started the row.

Fullerton, who had been voyeuristically in love with Colbert ever since seeing her movie *Torch Singer* in 1933, was immediately attracted to the picture. It showed the beautiful actress in a scene from the 1934 film *It Happened One Night* in which she had co-starred with Clark Gable and won an Oscar for best actress. Leaning across to the crewman who was immersed in the book, he slurred: 'I'd no mind screwin' that wee cow. Give us a look at tha book!'

The seaman ignored the remark and continued reading.

'Hey, I'm talkin' to ye. That Claudette Colbert is a right hot bit of stuff. Wha' she doin' in that story?'

The hulking reader looked up. 'Mind yer ain business, ye fookin' *bam-pot*,' he said in a Glasgow accent as thick as Fullerton's own.

Fired up by memories of watching the actress in the darkness of a Bridgeton cinema, not to mention sexual frustration and booze, Fullerton swung at the other man before Wilson or Mulholland could prevent him. It took several minutes to stop the mêlée and Fullerton found himself spending the rest of the journey nursing a painful black eye inflicted by the tougher Scotsman.

There were no further troubles on the voyage and Captain Bone watched the ship's anchor drop into the dark waters of the Canadian harbour with rather more optimism than when it had been lifted in New York. His mood was not, though, shared by the three Bridgeton boys – or many of the other Glaswegian recruits, for that matter – as they went ashore in Halifax for a second time. At least on this occasion, though, they knew what to expect, and where to go for a booze-up and where the fun was to be found.

Once all the men had gone ashore, Captain Bone and his officers could begin preparations for taking on board a total of 4,110 troops – officers, men and nursing sisters – to be conveyed to the UK. The commander even allowed himself a little smile as he walked through the troop quarters prior to the final inspection of the ship by the Canadian naval and military authorities. The work of the American dockyard team plus the fine-tuning and spit-and-polish of his own men had given the *George Washington* an altogether much smarter appearance than that conveyed by the rusting hulk he had first set eyes on in Philadelphia.

When the ship was given the all-clear and Captain Bone informed he could begin the embarkation, he was also handed a further piece of good news. The *George Washington* was to join a convoy leaving on 2 February and he was to be the commodore of the fleet.

The captain silently told himself that he was going home at last. All the misgivings he had nursed about the old ship seemed to have been misplaced. Or had they?

During the next hectic 24 hours, Captain Bone ordered his officers to get the massive task of taking on board over 4,000 people under way. The women were to be given the best quarters in what had formerly been the most luxurious area of the liner, while the men were accommodated in accordance with their rank: officers nearest the decks and other ranks below in descending order. The truth of the matter was, though, that the quality of the cabins and their furnishings was far better than any of the men or women might have expected on a normal troop transporter.

Once all the passengers were on board, and the 500 crew members at their posts, it merely required the inspecting brigadier of the Canadian Transport Authority to certify that everyone was suitably berthed and the *George Washington* could set sail. The message went down from the bridge to Archie Roberts to raise steam.

Then the nightmare began.

The sound of the steam as it blew from the escape pipes immediately told those who knew about such things that *something* was wrong. Very wrong. Listening to the sound, Captain Bone could not disguise his dismay. Later he wrote in his diary:

> There is nothing unusual in the purring of a feather of steam at the escape pipes when a ship is being brought to 'stand-by' for engine movements, but when the murmur mounts in crescendo to a tortured uproar and the sound takes the furious notes of the lash and crackling of multiple whips, then it is clear that the valves have been opened up and the high-pressure steam – so carefully raised and tended – is of purpose being thrown wide to the wind. With that din in my ears, I had no need to reach hastily for the engine-room telephone nor to await hopefully for the lessening of it that might denote a lifting of the safety-valves in trials.

As Captain Bone stared at the rush of blinding white steam, he knew the worst had happened. The boilers on which so much time and energy had already been spent had failed. When the chief engineer arrived on deck with a strained look on his face and his hands outspread in a gesture of resignation, there was no need for words between the two men.

Soon word of what had happened had spread among the passengers and crew. Now what? It was a situation that Captain Bone had not bargained for. And his disappointment was made all the more acute when he realised that he would not be able to command the convoy; the rest of the ships would have to leave without the *George Washington*.

The reaction of the three Bridgeton boys was quite different, however. The news had soon reached them that not one but two of the main boilers had developed cracks and there was evidence to suggest that one of the other boilers would not be able to stand up to the pressure. Another delay was inevitable – and one that would probably see them back on the loose in Halifax with more wages to spend.

The following morning, the boys' suspicions – and those of everyone else on board – were confirmed by a brief statement from Captain Bone, who had been wrestling with the problem throughout the night. The message was addressed to the whole ship's company. A Board of Enquiry would have to be set up to investigate the ship's failure and a new technical survey carried out into the boiler situation before anyone could contemplate bringing shipyard workers and welding plant on board. In the meantime, the fate of the 4,000 passengers had to be decided and non-essential members of the crew put ashore.

Snow had fallen during the night and left the ship's decks, masts and funnels swathed in white. As the captain and his officers began to grapple with their various assignments, and their passengers settled down to make themselves as comfortable as possible, several small groups of crew members crunched across the decks to await transportation to the city – among them those happy about the misfortune including John Wilson, Bill Fullerton and Paddy Mulholland.

They were determined to have a good time. Captain David Bone was equally determined the problems were not going to beat him. Unfortunately, the odds were now heavily stacked against him.

As soon as the Bridgeton trio were back in Halifax they began yet another round of drinking and renewing old acquaintanceships. A fellow crew member, Tommy O'Hara, who was also kept idle in the port while the ship was repaired once again, recalled that the boys, 'set off on a two-month rampage of crime and boozing'.

O'Hara, who was from Glasgow himself and had been a merchant seaman for ten years before signing on for the *George Washington*, had got to know the three gang members when they worked several shifts together. Although wary of the trio, he did find them good company in the ship's bar and their paths crossed several times during the enforced stay in Halifax.

According to O'Hara, stories about a number of ex-cons from Glasgow getting into trouble in the Canadian city became common knowledge and were remembered long after they had all left Canada. One particular episode involving Wilson, Fullerton and Mulholland stuck in the merchant seaman's mind:

> While we were in Halifax they opened this new mission hall for the merchant navy. It had been worked for and paid for by the people of the city and they got the famous English singer, Gracie Fields, to come and open it. She had apparently broken another engagement in New York to be there.
>
> In the normal way, I don't suppose the boys from Bridgeton would have gone except for the fact that they were advertising free booze for all seamen. But the organisers weren't going to serve any drinks until Gracie had done her bit. They wanted her to sing a few songs and then some members of the local committee made speeches thanking everybody.

Tommy O'Hara said that everyone kept quiet while Gracie sang, but then things got out of hand when it came to the speech-making:

The boys were thirsty and the longer the committee members went on the more impatient they became. They started muttering and when they were told to shut up, they became angry. Soon there was uproar in the place and the Bridgeton boys began brawling with some of the other seamen. The organisers managed to quieten things down and kicked the three men out without so much as a glass. I think Gracie Fields was pretty shaken up by the whole fracas.

O'Hara believes Wilson, Fullerton and Mulholland were also involved in another spot of bother that occurred during this period. It concerned an unidentified British naval officer, who, visiting the city, had a suitcase stolen as soon as he arrived at the CNR Station. O'Hara explained:

It contained his ceremonial uniform, and when the thieves who snatched it found out what was inside, they took the whole lot along to an auction and sold it, swords, medals and all. I was told the lot made about $650 and the gang then blew it all on a round of drinking in a beer tavern.

The Bridgeton boys were, in fact, very much in evidence again at the Beer Parlour near Duke Street and were certainly remembered there for spending like sailors on a spree. They were, though, as before, careful not to draw too much attention to themselves when the local policeman made his daily six o'clock call.

There is no actual evidence to link the boys from the *George Washington* to the reports of petty thieving in stores in Halifax, although the incidents bear all the hallmarks of their handiwork. During the month of February, the local papers, the *Chronicle-Herald* and *Mail-Star*, listed a number of unsolved crimes in shopping premises that diminished sharply after the ship had left port.

Old habits, of course, die hard. But considering their low wages and the limited proceeds of the theft of the naval officer's uniform – if the Bridgeton boys were, indeed, responsible – talk of a 'rampage of crime' is perhaps a little exaggerated.

Certainly, Captain Bone made no reference to troubles with his men on shore as he wrestled with the frustrating problems of his ship. Several meetings with the shipping experts had established that the three suspect boilers would require strengthening plates as well as extensive welding before the *George Washington* could proceed.

Another problem was the fact that the Halifax shipyards were packed with vessels requiring repairs and salvage work. Hardly a day passed without yet another ship limping in from the Atlantic with its superstructure holed or battered and its captain crying out for priority.

To their credit, the members of the Board of Enquiry carried out their preliminary inspection of the *George Washington* quickly and efficiently. But no date could be set for work to begin on the old liner; she would have to wait her turn in the queue. This left Captain Bone with another pressing decision to make. What to do with the 4,110 passengers?

It had taken just a single telephone call to the brigadier of the Canadian Transport Authority to establish that none of the troops, men or women, could be carried on any of the other ships in the convoy. These were already full to capacity and about to leave harbour for the Clyde. Nor was there a barracks or transit camp in Halifax to provide accommodation for such a large number of people. They would have to stay on board and then be embarked on to other ships as places became available.

Fortunately for Captain Bone – and these passengers – the *George Washington* had been fully provisioned for the Atlantic crossing and so there was no shortage of food and drink. The worry was that life on the ship might become difficult if the numbers had not decreased substantially by the time the repairs began. For then the lighting and heating would have to be reduced, even turned off, to facilitate welding. And all at a time of year when the temperature had already dropped virtually to zero.

However, thanks to some smart work by the Canadian authorities, the gradual dispersal of the troops took place. Meanwhile, day followed day of repairs and the days turned to weeks. To relieve the monotony, the troops were given permits to go into the city in small groups, but they always had to return to the ship to sleep.

This coming and going from the ship frequently caused congestion on the already congested harbour side. Tempers, too, became frayed on occasion under the stress of the extreme cold and the resurgence of some of the old animosity between merchant seamen and the armed forces invariably fuelled by drink. Bone noted at one point: 'During our period of immobility there were times of insubordination and loss of morale amongst the crew. For myself and the other officers there were seemingly endless plans and abortive arguments.'

When, finally, work did begin on the *George Washington*, Bone was somewhat surprised to discover that the expert welders who came on board were Americans from Baltimore. They did, though, immediately set to work with a will in what were far from ideal conditions.

The size of the old cruise liner meant she required a berth with deep water. Here the electricity had to come from a distant power station and the supply was occasionally interrupted and also suffered from leakages. Even the use of mobile 'boosters' to strengthen the flow of electricity did little to make the welders' work easier.

While he watched this work being carried out, Captain Bone wondered if he might be able to make a case for the installation of water-tube boilers in place of the existing damaged boilers. This idea had been mooted during the early days of the vessel's restoration at the League Island Yard in Philadelphia. But when Bone raised the idea with his superiors on the Navy Board in Ottawa, he was tersely informed that if such an extensive and expensive refit *had* been authorised, the ship would never have been transferred by the Americans but retained for their own service.

With the benefit of hindsight, it might be said that Captain Bone should have seen an omen in this statement. For, after two months of work on the boilers and after numerous tests, which all had to be studied and approved by the Naval Board, the final indignity fell upon him. He wrote in his log:

> When at last the work was completed and I reported to my superiors that the ship was ready for sea, it was only to learn that the voyage would be short. I was to take the *George Washington* to New York and there hand her back to the US Maritime Commissioners.

That, it seemed, was that. No explanation; no apologies for the delays or the inconveniences. Just a simple order in a few words putting an end to the whole saga. Captain Bone gave a sigh of resignation and ordered his officers to recall the crew.

The next morning, the harbour side was once again alive with seamen reporting back to the ship – among them three very bleary-eyed and hung-over Bridgeton boys. On board the *George Washington* they were all told that the ship was not sailing for the Clyde but returning to New York on 12 March. Until then there were shifts to be worked.

Despite their fuddled state, Wilson, Fullerton and Mulholland were still able to appreciate that these new orders were certainly better than facing the dangers of the Atlantic. They even promised a few more days boozing in the Big Apple. What they could not have foreseen was that the journey was to prove rather more hazardous than anyone imagined . . .

Ever since August 1941, the US Navy had been carrying out extensive operations between North America and Iceland keeping watch for marauding German U-boats. In what amounted to a state of undeclared war, Admiral Stark, the US chief of naval operations, had given explicit orders to his patrols to 'deal aggressively with any threat of attack' in the huge expanse of ocean considered to be American waters. The area was already familiarly known to merchant seamen as 'Torpedo Junction'.

An incident on 5 September of that year in which an American destroyer, the USS *Greer*, had depth-charged a German submarine, U-652, spotted by an observant aircraft pilot, signalled the beginning of US attacks on what President Roosevelt referred to as 'the rattlesnakes of the Atlantic'. The president added in a defiant broadcast to the nation that Hitler was now trying to 'destroy the bridge of ships which we are building across the Atlantic and over which we shall continue to roll the implements of war to help destroy him'. He promised the US Navy would now do its utmost to protect *all* the merchant ships of friendly nations in its waters.

Although the country was then still officially neutral, during the next three months US destroyers increasingly escorted merchant ships from North American harbours to the mid-Atlantic where they were passed on to the responsibility of the British Navy. The first American casualty following this policy occurred on 18 October when the destroyer *Kearny* was struck by a torpedo fired from U-568. The vessel was almost cut in half by the explosion, but still managed to limp to harbour in Iceland. On hearing the news that eleven crewmen had been killed – the first American naval casualties – Roosevelt angrily declared, 'The shooting war has started.'

Then, on 7 December, what had until now been a European war became a global conflict when Japanese planes bombed the American Pacific Fleet in Pearl Harbor. But the nation barely had time to draw breath after entering the war when trouble arrived on the doorstep with a vengeance. On 12 January a British merchantman, *Cyclops*, was sunk by a U-boat, 300 miles off Cape Cod, and the very next day another German submarine attacked and sank two freighters within sight of the harbour at Halifax.

Within hours of these attacks taking place, the American press was alive with rumours of hundreds of U-boats prowling off the East Coast, as Costello and Hughes have vividly described in their history of the Atlantic war:

> With few warships and aircraft available, there was little that could be done to police the 2,000 mile stretch of coastal waters from Maine to Florida. Facing public hysteria, the recently formed Eastern Sea Frontier's handful of Coastguard cutters and four Navy 'Blimp' airships were joined by 20 available aircraft; their wild goose chases followed hundreds of false sighting reports [*vide* the *George Washington* incident]. Apart from barring the broadcasts of weather forecasts, little could be done other than to share the hope of the *New York Times*, 'It is not believed that Germany could keep up widespread warfare of this sort.'

The truth of the matter was that they *could* and a wave of U-boats enjoyed rich pickings in the next two months off the American East Coast. Statistics show that over 430,000 tons of merchant shipping was sunk in February 1942 alone, with the success of these strikes causing the German media to crow loudly about 'The American Turkey Shoot' and Admiral Dönitz to claim that his submarines were now operating so close to the shore that 'bathers and sometimes entire cities are witness to that drama of war whose visual climaxes are constituted by the red glories of blazing vessels'.

It was against this background of a 'U-boat Blitz' – to quote one newspaper headline – that Captain David Bone set out in the *George Washington* from Halifax bound for New York on the evening of 12 March. If there was a crumb of comfort for the commander, it was the news that ten days earlier the US Navy had successfully depth-charged its first German submarine, the U-556, off Newfoundland.

The ship met heavy weather almost as soon as it had left the sanctuary of the Canadian harbour. And as the night drew on, it had to buck into a gale for several hours. As midnight passed, this gale subsided only to be followed by another. Some of the older seamen glanced at the calendar and realised it was now Friday the 13th.

Friday the 13th is a day of particular evil omen at sea, a date without luck according to the lore of the sea. As dawn broke, a full gale was blowing from the south-east. There was a high, crashing sea, rollers that lost their caps to the whipping wind and low, driving clouds. It was almost impossible to see anything through the spray and Captain Bone was pleased at how well the old liner rode the elements.

As the ship passed Cape Sable and headed across the great sweep of coastline running towards Boston, the storm began to subside. The weather cleared and well before she had reached Cape Cod, a stillness had settled over the ocean.

Captain Bone had read a report about the *Cyclops*, which had been sunk on this stretch of water, and urged his look-out to keep a careful watch on the grey seas now gently heaving around the boat as she continued at a steady fourteen knots. Below deck, the voices of the crew echoed along the corridors which were, of course, now deserted of any passengers. A few pairs of eyes even glanced apprehensively through the portholes as the vessel steamed on in the direction of Rhode Island.

Although the crew of the *George Washington* were not to know it at the time, there was, in fact, a U-boat in the vicinity, as subsequently captured records of the Germany Navy have revealed. U-130, with *Kapitanleutnant* Kals at the helm, was patrolling the ocean between Halifax and New York – the same submarine that had torpedoed the two ships off the Canadian coast in January.

Some of those on board the liner that anxious March morning were to swear for years after that they saw the outline of a submarine just below the surface, passing close by the ship. One story claimed that the boat was so close that the markings on the conning tower were visible to the naked eye. A trail of bubbles was also said to have marked the U-boat's passing.

What *is* certain is that there was no attack and Captain Bone made no mention of such an encounter in his log or his diary. If a U-boat had come that close to the *George Washington* it is almost inconceivable that it would not have attacked. A suggestion that because the liner had been built in Germany it might have been mistaken as a friendly ship is hardly credible.

That night the ship reached the safety of New York and Captain Bone ordered the anchor to be dropped in the harbour for the last time – at least as far as he was concerned. The following day his command of the *George Washington* – which had lasted eight months with scarcely a month of those at sea – came to a prosaic end when he handed her over to a representative of the US Maritime Commissioners. It had been a bizarre, frustrating and even dangerous adventure that had probably cost the British government a fortune without any return as well as being Captain Bone's most unusual command.

It is doubtful whether the captain saw the troublesome crew members Wilson, Fullerton and Mulholland leave the ship for the last time. They were no doubt bent on spending more days and nights in the bars of New York before perhaps taking up an offer of another boat back to the UK. The facts about their subsequent lives are altogether unclear.

It is probable that Wilson and Fullerton did join another merchant ship and returned to the Clyde in the July of that year, although a search of the crew lists of this period provides no such names. They may even have been among a number of the Glasgow hardmen who were subsequently reported to have enjoyed the life of the merchant seaman and remained in the profession for the duration of the war. As Tommy O'Hara, one of the last contacts with the *George Washington*, put it:

> I heard that some of the crew earned fine war records. But some of the others found another kind of fame in the Glasgow underworld. Whatever they did, I don't suppose any of them forget their time on what we used to refer to as 'the jail that went to sea.'

The strangest story of all, however, concerns the final member of the Bridgeton boys, young Paddy Mulholland. He is believed to have stayed in New York and served for a time in what was aptly known as the 'Hooligans' Navy'.

In their desire to combat the U-boat menace along the East Coast during the spring of 1942, the US Navy Department instituted an urgent programme of building more anti-submarine coastal craft using the slogan 'Sixty Ships in Sixty Days'. While the Navy waited for these destroyers and patrol boats to arrive, they accepted all sorts of offers of help, including one from the Cruising Club of America. This nautical organisation presented the Navy with thirty auxiliary sailing vessels, all to be manned by volunteers.

Mulholland, who had by now decided to stay in America like McCormack and McCourt before him, is thought to have volunteered to serve on one of the boats. Although the men were all volunteers, they were well paid and lavished with plenty to eat and drink between missions.

The life was one that would undoubtedly have suited Mulholland with his passion for the sea. And the evidence that he *did* serve is given credibility by the discovery of the name, 'Mulholland, P' among the lists of those who belonged to the 'Hooligan's Navy'.

His contribution was, though, very likely similar to the part he played in the saga of the *George Washington*. For a report published after the war states: 'The "Hooligans' Navy" primarily carried out the duty of pickets off the harbours of the East Coast. Their efforts were good for public morale, but did little to stop the U-boats.'

Epilogue

The fortunes of the *George Washington* took a dramatic upturn after she was handed back to the US Maritime Commission by Captain David Bone in March 1942.

Two months later, in June, she was sent to Todd's Brooklyn Yard in New York and fitted with the new boilers that Captain Bone had believed could be the solution to her problems. These were water-tube boilers which burned oil instead of coal and enabled her to maintain and even better the speed her erstwhile British captain had striven to achieve.

As a result of this refit, the vessel was now capable of speeds of eighteen knots and could travel 12,000 miles at that rate. During the work in New York, one of her funnels had also been taken away to improve her aerodynamics, and the removal of the now redundant coal bunkers also freed up still more space for troop carrying.

When the *George Washington* once again put to sea early in 1943, she was able to accommodate up to 5,000 US Army men in comfort. Under her new master, Captain John Batchelder, she then made a series of successful journeys to and from the Far East during the next three years.

On one visit to Bombay in October 1943, she was berthed by pure chance at Ballard Pier near a British ship, the H.M.S. *Circassia*. The ship was captained by none other than David

Bone. It was a surprising and emotional moment for the veteran sailor still plying his trade. He was pleased to see the boat that had given him so many agonies, 'back in the water, as I had known she would be, a grand "sea boat"'.

But tragedy was ultimately destined to be the lot of the *George Washington*. In March 1947 while in New York she was badly damaged by fire and had to be taken away and laid up in Baltimore. Four years later, on 17 January 1951, another fire broke out on the quay, which spread rapidly and completely destroyed the once great luxury liner. The wreckage was scrapped until not a trace remained.

The Battle of the Atlantic, in which it was planned the *George Washington* would play a part, reached a turning point in 1943. By then technological advances in undersea surveillance and extended air cover had enabled the escorts taking merchant ships across the ocean finally to gain the upper hand against the U-boats.

The losses, though, had been heavy. Nearly 2,500 Allied merchant ships were sunk and of the 30,000 merchant seamen lost at sea, the overwhelming majority were killed in the conflict on the Atlantic Ocean. The cost to the German submarines was equally high – by the end of the war 28,000 crewmen had been lost, with a casualty rate of more than sixty per cent.

Captain David Bone continued to serve with distinction on merchant ships until the end of the war when he retired from the sea. In 1946 he was knighted for his services to the merchant navy and went to live with his wife in Tilford, on the picturesque North Downs in Surrey.

In the remaining years of his life he devoted himself to writing: contributing to various periodicals, producing a novel, *The Queerfella* (1952), and a memoir of his time afloat, *Landfall at Sunset* (1955). The rest of the time David Bone followed 'country pursuits' – as he put it in his entry in *Who's Who* – all of them a world away from his earlier life at sea. He died on 17 May 1959.

The five Bridgeton boys, John Wilson, William McCormack, Bill Fullerton, Bobbie McCourt and Paddy Mulholland, were never heard of again.

Bibliography

Books

Adams, Samuel Hopkins. *It Happened One Night* (Longmans, 1934).

Bennet, C. L. & Filion, Gerald. *The Face of Canada* (Clarke, Irwin & Co, 1960).

Bone, Captain David W. *The Brassbounder* (Gerald Duckworth & Co, 1910).

— *Merchantman Rearmed* (Chatto & Windus, 1949).

Churchill, Winston S. *The Second World War* (Cassell, 1962).

Cockerill, A. W. *Sir Percy Sillitoe* (W. H. Allen, 1975).

Conrad, Joseph. *Suspense* (J. M. Dent, 1927).

Costello, John & Hughes, Terry. *Battle of the Atlantic* (Collins, 1977).

Creighton, Kenelm. *Convoy Commodore* (Michael Joseph, 1956).

Daiches, David. *Glasgow* (Andre Deutsch, 1977).

Dear, I. C. & Foot, M. R. D. *Oxford Companion to the Second World War* (OUP, 1995).

Divine, A. D. *The Merchant Navy Fights: Tramps Against U-Boats* (Bles, 1941).

Hanley, Clifford. *Dancing in the Streets* (Faber, 1958).

Kludas, Arnold. *Great Passenger Ships of the World* (Patrick Stephens, 1976).

Knox, Collie. *Atlantic Battle* (Hutchinson, 1943).

Lindsey, Maurice. *Portrait of Glasgow* (Robert Hale, 1972).

Macintyre, Donald. *The Battle of the Atlantic* (Batsford, 1961).

McGhee, Bill. *Cut and Run* (Corgi, 1963).

Oakley, C. A. *The Second City* (Cape, 1946).

Patrick James. *A Glasgow Gang Observed* (Eyre Methuen, 1973).

Repplier, Agnes. *Philadelphia: The Place and the People* (Macmillan, 1938).

Sillitoe, P. *Cloak Without Dagger* (Cassell, 1955).

Thompson, Julian. *The War at Sea* (Sidgwick & Jackson, 1996).

Young, John M. *Britain's Sea War: A Diary of Ship Losses 1939–1945* (Patrick Stephens, 1989).

Newspapers & Documents

Daily Herald

Daily Mail

Daily Record

Daily Telegraph

Glasgow Evening Citizen

Glasgow Evening News

Glasgow Evening Times

Glasgow Herald

Halifax Chronicle-Herald

Halifax Mail-Star

Lloyd's Register

Montreal Matin

Montreal Star

New Society

New York Daily News

New York Post

New York Times

News of the World

People's Journal

Philadelphia Daily News

Philadelphia Evening Public Ledger

Red Poppy Magazine

Sunday Chronicle

Sunday Express

Sunday Pictorial

The Sunday Mail

The Times

Yorkshire Telegraph & Star

American Naval Institute, Washington; British Museum, London; Corporation of Glasgow Housing Management Department; Glasgow Police Records Department; Library of Congress, Washington; Public Record Office, Richmond, Surrey; Scottish Prison Service, Barlinnie; US Navy Department Archives.

Acknowledgements

There are a great many people who have helped in the research and writing of this book, none more so than my late friend, Bill Lofts, who would, I am sure, be pleased to see the remarkable story that he first investigated half a century ago at last in print. I should like to couple his name with that of Peter Hawkins, Jim McGarrity, George Crawford, Pat Docherty, Rona Sweeney and Chris Scott, as well as my publisher, Jeremy Robson, for commissioning the book and my excellent editors, Jane Donovan and Sarah Barlow. Nor must I forget the ever-friendly and helpful librarians at The London Library, The British Newspaper Library, Colindale and the Library of Congress in Washington, DC.

Index

Index

Index